AMERICAN LANGUAGE
REPRINTS

VOL. 23

THE
TUTELO
LANGUAGE

by
Horatio Hale

Evolution Publishing
Merchantville, New Jersey

Reprinted from:

Horatio Hale. 1883. "The Tutelo Tribe and Language".
Proceedings of the American Philosophical Society
21 (114):1-47.

This edition ©2001 by Evolution Publishing.
an imprint of Arx Publishing, LLC

Originally published in hardcover 2001.
Reprinted in paperback 2021.

Printed in the
United States of America

ISBN 978-1-935228-21-9

CONTENTS

Preface to the 2001 edition

In the year 1753 the Five Nations of the Iroquois admitted into their famed confederacy the remnants of a people they called the "Tedarighroones." These had originally lived in the foothills of the Virginia mountains, where they suffered attacks at the Iroquois' hands during the Beaver Wars of the late 1600's. Around 1712 the various survivors regrouped and sought protection from Governor Spotswood of Virginia, who settled them near Fort Christanna, where, however, the attacks continued until a peace treaty was finally signed in 1722. But within a very short time the "Tedarighroones", or the Tutelo as they were later known, were experiencing mistreatments anew, this time from the English colonists in Virginia. Around 1740 they left Fort Christanna and, in an ironic reversal of fortune, settled in Pennsylvania under the protection of their former enemies the Iroquois, with whom they have resided ever since.

For over a hundred years the scholarly world knew nothing of the cultural affiliations of the Tutelo tribe save that they were under the protection of the Five Nations. Then in 1870 a scholar named Horatio Hale visited the last remaining full blooded member of the tribe and recorded from him a vocabulary which proved beyond doubt the Siouan affiliation of their language. This came as a surprise to Hale and others as well, for the Siouans had always been known exclusively as a tribe of the Plains, and no one had any inkling that their family could have extended this far to the east. But as Hale's discovery

1

was made known (e.g. Anderson 1871), the Siouan presence in the Atlantic states could no longer be doubted, and the prehistory of Siouan-speaking nations was now cast in a whole new light.

It is generally accepted today that the Virginia Siouans were descended mainly from the Monacan and Manahoac confederacies described by John Smith in the early 1600's. These groups encompassed a number of individual towns, one of which was that of the Tutelo, although there is some disagreement where the town was originally located, whether along the Big Sandy River in West Virginia (Swanton 1936, 1943) or somewhat further east along the Dan river, where the explorers Batts and Fallam found a "Totera" town in 1671.

In any case, by the time the Virginia Siouan remnants had gathered at Fort Christanna, they had become a melting pot of five tribes: Tutelo, Saponi, Occaneechi, Stenkenock, and Meipontsky, the first three of which seem to have been the most important. The early sources often referred to them all as "Saponis" until the Iroquois-derived "Tutelo" became more prominent; at times they were also simply called "Christanna Indians." The Occaneechi must also have had some degree of prominence, since Robert Beverley in his *History and Present State of Virginia* (1705) recounts that despite their being a small nation, their language was "understood by the chief Men of many Nations."

The explorer John Lederer specifically attested to the presence of various dialects amoung the Virginia Siouan tribes (Mooney 1894, p. 29), but linguistics has not yet confirmed what dialect differences originally existed, if any, among the groups at Christanna. Scholars have generally circumvented the question by simply referring to the language as "Tutelo-Saponi", or simply "Tutelo" with Saponi and Occaneechi understood (Goddard 1996, p. 8).

Tutelo-Saponi's position within the wider Siouan family is quite clear: it belongs to the Ohio Valley or Southeastern subgroup of Siouan. Its two closest linguistic relatives, Ofo and Biloxi, were both first recorded—incongruously—in Louisiana. However, these tribes seem to have originally resided in the Ohio Valley until being driven down the Ohio and Mississippi by the Iroquois sometime in the mid-1600's. (Swanton 1943; for a more skeptical view see Griffin 1943, Hunter 1978) Some scholars (Swanton 1936, Voegelin 1941) have even made the case that the Ohio Valley was the original homeland of all the Siouan-speaking peoples, but this view has not been universally accepted (e.g. Griffin 1942). It is not an easy issue to settle since we know very little about the original inhabitants of the Ohio Valley, but "chances are good that one or more of these groups spoke a Siouan language" (Goddard 1978b).

Documentation of the Tutelo-Saponi language is not extensive. The early part of the 20th century saw the publication of two salvage vocabularies (Sapir 1913, Frachtenberg 1913) taken from Tutelo speakers who remembered only a few fragments of their ancestral language. Not much has been recorded of the Saponi dialect either: a handful of translated creek names, and a 40-word vocabulary from Fort Christanna, a portion of which is actually Algonquian and may record the trade language of the Occaneechi (Goddard 1978a).

But by far the most significant contribution to the study of Tutelo-Saponi was the one made by Horatio Hale himself based on his interviews with the Tutelo remnants at Six Nations Reserve. Most of the details are better explained by Hale's own introduction, so we will only summarize the main points here.

Hale's description of Tutelo first appeared in the *Proceedings of the American Philosophical Society* for 1883, but the actual data was collected during and after 1870 on the Six Nations Reserve near Brantford, Ontario. Hale's primary informant was Nikonha or "Old Mosquito", the last full blooded Tutelo; two other informants were also consulted and contributed particularly to the grammatical section: a half-Tutelo chief and his elderly aunt. Hale tells us he worked from a questionnaire modeled on that drawn up in the 1820's by Albert Gallatin for his *Synopsis of the Indian Tribes* (1836), but added a number of additional words "expressive of the most common objects or actions." Perhaps his most important contribution, however, was not the vocabulary itself, but rather his extensive grammatical notes—the only such treatment of Tutelo ever published.

For this new edition the text of Hale's article has been reprinted in full, while the vocabulary section has been adapted to the format of the present series. The original vocabulary was printed as a table, listing the English terms alphabetically on the leftmost column, followed by their respective Tutelo, Dakota and Hidatsa equivalents in subsequent columns. The comparative Dakota and Hidatsa terms, while preserved in the grammatical section, have been left out of the vocabulary section. An alphabetical Tutelo-English section has been added to the English-Tutelo, with all the variants given by Hale listed individually as separate headwords. All abbreviations and diacritical marks have been preserved; explanations of them can be found on page 33 and following.

The numbers of the Tutelo continued to dwindle throughout the late 1800's. Hale tells us that one of his informants was called "chief" and exercised his prerogative under Iroquois law to address the council in his native tongue, but only because he was "allowed to retain his seat after his constituency had disappeared" and not because there was any significant Tutelo community to lead at Six Nations Reserve. Frachtenberg (1913) visited the reservation in 1907, to find only two Tutelo families left there: the Williams family, who remembered nothing of the language, and the Buck family, who along with a Cayuga named Andrew Sprague, were its last speakers.

Soon afterwards, the final vestiges of Tutelo-Saponi as a living language were extinguished forever. But thanks to the efforts of Hale and other scholars, some of its basic structure and vocabulary have been preserved for future generations to study and enjoy.

—Claudio R. Salvucci, series ed.

Bibliography and Recommended Reading

Anderson, Rev. Joseph. 1871. The newly discovered relationship of the Tuteloes to the Dakotan stock. *Proceedings of the American Philological Association*, Third ann. sess., p. 15-16. July 26, 1871.

Carter, Richard T. 1980. "The Woccon language of North Carolina: its genetic affiliations and historical significance". *International Journal of American Linguistics* 46 (3):170-182.

Foster, Michael K. 1996. "Language and the culture history of North America." in William Sturtevant, Ives Goddard, eds., *Handbook of North American Indians vol. 17: Languages*, pp. 64-110, esp. "Siouan-Catawba" pp.100-104. Washington D.C.:Smithsonian Institution.

Frachtenberg, Leo. 1913. "Contributions to a Tutelo Vocabulary." *American Anthropologist*, n.s. 15(3):477-479.

Gallatin, Albert. 1836. "A Synopsis of the Indian Tribes of North America". in *Archaeologia Americana: Transactions and Collections of the American Antiquarian Society, vol. 2*. Cambridge:University Press.

Goddard, Ives. 1978a. "Eastern Algonquian Languages." in William Sturtevant, Bruce Trigger, eds., *Handbook of North American Indians vol. 15: Northeast*, pp. 70-77. Washington D.C.:Smithsonian Institution.

Goddard, Ives. 1978b. "Central Algonquian Languages." in William Sturtevant, Bruce Trigger, eds., *Handbook of North American Indians vol. 15: Northeast*, pp. 583-587. Washington D.C.:Smithsonian Institution.

Goddard, Ives. 1996. "The classification of the native languages of North America." in William Sturtevant, Ives Goddard, eds., *Handbook of North American Indians vol. 17: Languages,* pp. 290-323. Washington D.C.:Smithsonian Institution.

Griffin, James B. 1942. "On the Historic Location of the Tutelo and the Mohetan in the Ohio Valley." *American Anthropologist*, n.s. 44(2)275-280.

Griffin, James B. 1943. *The Fort Ancient Aspect, its Cultural and Chronological Position in Mississippi Valley Archaeology*. Ann Arbor:University of Michigan Press.

Gruber, Jacob W. 1967. "Horatio Hale and the development of American Anthropology." *Proceedings of the American Philosophical Society* 111:5-37. Philadelphia.

Hunter, William A. 1978. "History of the Ohio Valley." in William Sturtevant, Bruce Trigger, eds., *Handbook of North American Indians vol. 15: Northeast*, pp. 588-593. Washington D.C.:Smithsonian Institution.

Mooney, James. 1894. The Siouan tribes of the east. *Bureau of American Ethnology Bulletin* 157.

Sapir, Edward. 1913. "A Tutelo Vocabulary." *American Anthropologist*, n.s. 15(2):295-297.

Sturtevant, William C. 1958. "Siouan languages in the east". *American Anthropologist* 60 (4):738-743.

Swanton, John R. 1936. "Early History of the Eastern Siouan Tribes." in Robert H. Lowie, ed., *Essays in Anthropology Presented to A. L. Kroeber,* pp. 371-381. Berkeley:University of California Press.

Swanton, John R. 1943. "Siouan Tribes of the Ohio Valley." *American Anthropologist*, n.s. 45(1):49-66.

Voegelin, C. F. 1941. "Internal relationships of Siouan languages." *American Anthropologist* 43:246-49.

The Tutelo Tribe and Language
by Horatio Hale

(Read before the American Philosophical Society March 2, 1883.)

The tribes of the Dakota stock, under various designations—Osages, Quappas, Kansas, Otoes, Omahas, Minitarees (or Hidatsas), Iowas, Mandans, Sioux (or Dakotas proper) and Assiniboins, have always been regarded as a people of the western prairies, whose proper home was the vast region lying west of the Mississippi, and stretching from the Arkansas River on the south to the Saskatchawan on the north. A single tribe, the Winnebagoes, who dwelt east of the Mississippi, near the western shore of Lake Michigan, were deemed to be intruders into the territory of the Algonkin nations. The fact, which has been recently ascertained, that several tribes speaking languages of the Dakota stock were found by the earliest explorers occupying the country east of the Alleghenies, along a line extending through the southern part of Virginia and the northern portion of North Carolina, nearly to the Atlantic ocean, has naturally awakened much interest. This interest will be heightened if it shall appear that not only must our ethnographical maps of North America be modified but that a new element has been introduced into the theory of Indian migrations. Careful researches seem to show that while the language of these eastern tribes is closely allied to that of the western Dakotas, it bears evidence of being older in form. If this conclusion shall be verified, the supposition, which at first was natural, that these eastern tribes were merely offshoots of the Dakota stock, must be deemed at least improbable. The course of migration may be found to have followed the contrary direction, and the western Dakotas, like the western Algonkins, may find their parent stock in the east. As a means of solving this interesting problem, the study of the history and language of a tribe now virtually extinct assumes a peculiar scientific value. Philologists will notice, also, that in this study there is presented to them a remarkable instance of an inflected language closely allied in its vocabulary and in many of its forms to dialects which are mainly agglutinative in their structure, and bear but slight traces of inflection.

In the year 1671 an exploring party under Captain Batt, leaving "the Apomatock Town," on the James River, penetrated into the mountains of Western Virginia, at a distance, by the route they traveled, of two hundred and fifty miles from their starting point. At this point they found "the Tolera Town in a very rich swamp between a breach [branch] and the main river of the Roanoke, circled about by mountains."* There are many errata in the printed narrative, and the circumstances leave no doubt that "Tolera" should be "Totera." On their way to this town the party had passed the Sapong [Sapony] town, which, according to the journal, was about one hundred and fifty miles west of the Apomatock Town, and about a hundred miles east of the "Toleras." A few years later we shall find these tribes in closer vicinity and connection.

At this period the Five Nations were at the height of their power, and in the full flush of that career of conquest

*Batt's *Journal and Relation of a New Discovery* in N. Y. Hist. Col. Vol. iii, p. 191.

which extended their empire from the Georgian Bay on the north to the Roanoke River on the south. They had destroyed the Hurons and the Eries, had crushed the Andastes (or Conestoga Indians), had reduced the Delawares to subjection, and were now brought into direct collision with the tribes of Virginia and the Carolinas. The Toteras (whom we shall henceforth know as the Tuteloes) began to feel their power. In 1686 the French missionaries had occasion to record a projected expedition of the Senecas against a people designated in the printed letter the "Tolere,"—the same misprint occurring once more in the same publication."† The traditions of the Tuteloes record long continued and destructive wars waged against them and their allies by the Iroquois, and more especially by the two western nations, the Cayugas and Senecas. To escape the incursions of their numerous and relentless enemies, they retreated further to the south and east. Here they came under the observation of a skilled explorer, John Lawson, the Surveyor-General of South Carolina. In 1701, Lawson traveled from Charleston, S. C., to Pamlico sound. In this journey he left the sea-coast at the mouth of the Santee river, and pursued a northward course into the hilly country, whence he turned eastward to Pamlico. At the Sapona river, which was the west branch of the Cape Fear or Clarendon river, he came to the Sapona town, where he was well received.‡ He there heard of the Toteros as "a neighboring nation" in the "western mountains." "At that

---

† Lambreville to Bruyas, Nov. 4, 1686 in N. Y. Hist. Col., Vol. iii, p. 484.
‡ Gallatin suggests that Lawson was here in error, and that the Sapona river was a branch of the Great Pedee, which he does not mention, and some branches which he evidently mistook for tributaries of the Cape Fear river.—*Synopsis of the Indian Tribes* p. 86.

time," he adds, "these Toteros, Saponas, and the Keyawees, three small nations, were going to live together, by which they thought they should strengthen themselves and become formidable to their enemies."

They were then at war with the powerful and dreaded Senecas—whom Lawson styles Sinnagers. While he was at the Sapona town, some of the Toteras warriors came to visit their allies. Lawson was struck with their appearance. He describes them, in his quaint idiom, as "tall, likely men, having great plenty of buffaloes, elks and bears, with every sort of deer, amongst them, which strong food makes large, robust bodies." In another place he adds: "These five nations of the Toteros, Saponas, Keiauwees, Aconechos and Schoicories are lately come amongst us, and may contain in all about 750 men, women and children."* It is known that the Toteroes (or Tuteloes) and Saponas understood each other's speech, and it is highly probable that all the five tribes belonged to the same stock. They had doubtless fled together from southwestern Virginia before their Iroquois invaders. The position in which they had taken refuge might well have seemed to them safe, as it placed between them and their enemies the strong and warlike Tuscarora nation, which numbered then, according to Lawson's estimate, twelve hundred warriors, clustered in fifteen towns, stretching along the Neuse and Tar rivers. Yet, even behind this living rampart, the feeble confederates were not secure. Lawson was shown, near the Sapona town, the graves of seven Indians who had been lately killed by the "Sinnegars or Jennitos"—names by which Gallatin

---

* Lawson's "History of Carolina;" reprinted by Strother & Marcom. Raleigh, 1860 ; p. 384.

understands the Senecas and Oneidas, though as regards the latter identification there may be some question.

The noteworthy fact mentioned by Lawson, that buffaloes were found in "great plenty" in the hilly country on the head waters of the Cape Fear river, may be thought to afford a clue to the causes which account for the appearance of tribes of Dakota lineage east of the Alleghenies. The Dakotas are peculiarly a hunting race, and the buffalo is their favorite game. The fact that the Big Sandy river, which flows westward from the Alleghenies to the Ohio, and whose head waters approach those of the Cape Fear river, was anciently known as the Totteroy river, has been supposed to afford an indication that the progress of the Toteros or Tutelos, and perhaps of the buffaloes which they hunted, may be traced along its course from the Ohio valley eastward. There are evidences which seem to show that this valley was at one time the residence, or at least the hunting ground, of tribes of the Dakota stock. Gravier (in 1700) affirms that the Ohio river was called by the Illinois and the Miamis the Akansea river, because the Akanseas formerly dwelt along it.† The Akanseas were identical with the Quappas, and have at a later day given their name to the river and State of Arkansas. Catlin found reason for believing that the Mandans, another tribe of the Southern Dakota stock, formerly—and at no very distant period—resided in the valley of the Ohio. The peculiar traces in the soil which

† "Elle" (the Ohio) "s'appelle par les Illinois et par les Oumiamis la riv-ière des Akanseas, parceque les Akanseas l'habitoient autrefois."— Gravier, Relation de Voyage, p.10. I am indebted for this and other references to my esteemed friend, Dr. J. G. Shea, whose unsurpassed knowledge of Indian history is not more admirable than the liberality with which its stores are placed at the command of his friends.

13

marked the foundations of their dwellings and the position of their villages were evident, he affirms, at various points along that river. It is by no means improbable that when the buffalo abounded on the Ohio, the Dakota tribes found its valley their natural home, and that they receded with it to the westward of the Mississippi. But the inference that the region west of the Mississippi was the original home of the Dakotas, and that those of that stock who dwelt on the Ohio or east of the Alleghenies were emigrants from the Western prairies, does not, by any means, follow. By the same course of reasoning we might conclude that the Aryans had their original seat In Western Europe, that the Portuguese were emigrants from Brazil, and that the English derived their origin from America. The migrations of races are not to be traced by such recent and casual vestiges. The only evidence which has real weight in any inquiry respecting migrations in prehistoric times is that of language; and where this fails, as it sometimes does, the question must be pronounced unsoluble.

The protection which the Tuteloes had received from the Tuscaroras and their allies soon failed them. In the year 1711 a war broke out between the Tuscaroras and the Carolina settlers, which ended during the following year in the complete defeat of the Indians. After their overthrow the great body of the Tuscaroras retreated northward and joined the Iroquois, who received them into their league as the sixth nation of the confederacy. A portion, however, remained near their original home. They merely retired a short distance northward into the Virginian territory, and took up their abode in the tract

14

which lies between the Roanoke and the Potomac rivers. Here they were allowed to remain at peace, under the protection of the Virginian government. And here they were presently joined by the Tuteloes and Saponas, with their confederates. In September, 1722, the governors of New York, Pennsylvania, and Virginia, held a conference at Albany with the chiefs of the Iroquois, to endeavor to bring about a peace between them and the southern tribes. On this occasion Governor Spotteswood, of Virginia, enumerated the tribes for which the government or his Province would undertake to engage. Among them were certain tribes which were commonly known under the name of the "Christanna Indians," a name derived from that of a fort which had been established in their neighborhood. These were "the Saponies, Ochineeches, Stenkenoaks, Meipontskys, and Toteroes," all of whom, it appears, the Iroquois were accustomed to comprehend under the name of Todirichrones.*

Some confusion and uncertainty, however, arise in consulting the colonial records of this time, from the fact that this name of Todirichrones was applied by the Iroquois to two distinct tribes, or rather confederacies, of Southern Indians, belonging to different stocks, and speaking languages totally dissimilar. These were, on the one hand, the Tuteloes (or Toteroes) and their allies, and, on the other, the powerful Catawba nation. The Catawbas occupied the eastern portion of the Carolinas, south of the Tuscarora nation. At the beginning of the last century they numbered several thousand souls. As late as 1743, according to Adair, they could still muster four

* N. Y. Hist. Col., Vol. v, p. 655 et seq.

hundred warriors. A bitter animosity existed between them and the Iroquois, leading to frequent hostilities which the English authorities at this conference sought to repress. It was the policy of the Iroquois, from ancient times, always to yield to overtures of peace from any Indian nation. On this occasion they responded in their usual spirit. "Though there is among you," they replied to the Virginians, "a nation, the Todirichrones, against whom we have had so inveterate an enmity that we thought it could only be extinguished by their total extirpation, yet, since you desire it, we are willing to receive them into this peace, and to forget all the past."*

The Catawba language is a peculiar speech, differing widely if not radically, both from the Dakota and from the Iroquois languages.† The only connection between the Catawbas and the Tuteloes appears to have arisen from the fact that they were neighboring and perhaps politically allied tribes, and were alike engaged in hostilities with the Iroquois. The latter, however, seem to have confounded them all together, under the name of the tribe

* N. Y. Hist. Col., Vol. v, p. 660.

† Gallatin, in his Synopsis classes the Catawba as a separate stock, distinct from the Dakota. The vocabulary which he gives seems to warrant this separation, the resemblances of words being few and of a doubtful character. On the other hand, in the first annual report of the Bureau of Ethnology connected with the Smithsonian Institution (Introduction, p. xix) the Kataba (or Catawba) is ranked among the languages of the Dakotan family. My esteemed correspondent, Mr. A. S. Gatschet, whose extensive acquaintance with Indian linguistics gives great weight to his opinion on any subject connected with this study, informs me (March 31, 1882) that this classification was conjectural and provisional, and that his subsequent researches among the few survivors of the tribe have not yet resulted in confirming it. They show certain traces of resemblance, both in the vocabulary and the syntax, but too slight and distant to make the affiliation certain. We shall have, as he remarks, "to compare more material, or more attentively that which we have, to arrive at a final result."

which lay nearest to the confederacy and was the best known to them.

One result of the peace thus established was that the Tuteloes and Saponas, after a time, determined to follow the course which had been taken by the major portion of their Tuscarora friends, and place themselves directly under the protection of the Six Nations. Moving northward across Virginia, they established themselves at Shamokin (since named Sunbury) in what is now the centre of Pennsylvania. It was a region which the Iroquois held by right of conquest, its former occupants, the Delawares and Shawanese, having been either expelled or reduced to subjection. Here, under the shadow of the great confederacy, many fragments of broken tribes were now congregated — Conoys, Nanticokes, Delawares, Tuteloes, and others.

In September, 1745, the missionary, David Brainerd, visited Shamokin. He describes it in his diary as containing upwards of fifty houses and nearly three hundred persons. "They are," he says, "of three different tribes of Indians, speaking three languages wholly unintelligible to each other. About one half of its inhabitants are Delawares, the others Senekas and Tutelas."* Three years later, in the summer of 1748, an exploring party of Moravian missionaries passed through the same region. The celebrated Zeisberger, who was one of them, has left a record of their travels. From this we gather that the whole of the Tuteloes were not congregated in Shamokin. Before reaching that town, they passed through Skogari, in what is now Columbia county. In Zeisberger's biography the impression formed of this town by the travelers is expressed in

* Life of Brainerd, p. 167, Am. Tract Soc. edition. Quoted in the "Life of Zeisberger," by De Schweinitz, p. 71.

17

brief but emphatic terms. It was "the only town on the continent inhabited by Tuteloes, a degenerate remnant of thieves and drunkards."† This disparaging description was perhaps not unmerited. Yet some regard must be paid to a fact of which the good missionary could not be aware, namely, that the Indians who are characterized in these unsavory terms belonged to a stock distinguished from the other Indians whom he knew by certain marked traits of character. Those who are familiar with the various branches of the Indian race are aware that every tribe, and still more every main stock, or ethnic family, has certain special characteristics, both physical and mental. The Mohawk differs in look and character decidedly from the Onondaga, the Delaware from the Shawanese, the Sioux from the Mandan; and between the great divisions to which these tribes belong, the differences are much more strongly marked. The Iroquois have been styled "the Romans of the West." The designation is more just than is usual in such comparisons. Indeed, the resemblance between these great conquering communities is strikingly marked. The same politic forethought in council, the same respect for laws and treaties, the same love of conquest, the same relentless determination in war, the same clemency to the utterly vanquished, a like readiness to strengthen their power by the admission of strangers to the citizenship, an equal reliance on strong fortifications, similar customs of forming outlying colonies, and of ruling subject nations by proconsular deputies, a similar admixture of aristocracy and democracy in their constitution, a like taste for agriculture, even a notable similarity in the strong and heavy mould of figure

† Life of Zeisberger, by De Schweinitz, p. 149.

and the bold and massive features, marked the two peoples who, on widely distant theatres of action, achieved not dissimilar destinies.

Pursuing the same classical comparison, we might liken the nearest neighbors of the Iroquois, the tribes of the Algonkin stock, whose natural traits are exemplified in their renowned sachems, Powhatan, Philip of Pokanoket, Miantanomah, Pontiac, and Tecumseh, to the ingenious and versatile Greeks, capable of heroism, but incapable of political union, or of long-sustained effort. A not less notable resemblance might be found between the wild and wandering Scythians of old, and the wild and wandering tribes of the great Dakotan stock. Reckless and rapacious, untamable and fickle, fond of the chase and the fight, and no less eager for the dance and the feast, the modern Dakotas present all the traits which the Greek historians and travelers remarked in the barbarous nomads who roamed along their northern and eastern frontiers.

The Tuteloes, far from the main body of their race, and encircled by tribes of Algonkin and Iroquois lineage, showed all the distinctive characteristics of the stock to which they belonged. The tall, robust huntsmen of Lawson, chasers of the elk and the deer, had apparently degenerated, half a century later, into a "remnant of thieves and drunkards," at least as seen in the hurried view of a passing missionary. But it would seem that their red-skinned neighbors saw in them some qualities which gained their respect and liking. Five years after Zeisberger's visit, the Iroquois, who had held them hitherto under a species of tutelage, decided to admit them, together with their fellow-refugees, the Algonkin Nanticokes from the Eastern Shore of Maryland, to the full honors of the confederacy. The step received the commendation of so shrewd a judge as Colonel (afterwards Sir William) Johnson. At a great council of the Six Nations, held at Onondaga in September, 1758, Colonel Johnson congratulated the Cayugas on the resolution they had formed of "strengthening their castle" by taking in the Tedarighroones.* At about the same time a band of Delawares was received into the League. When a great council was to be convened in 1756, to confer with Colonel Johnson on the subject of the French war, wampum belts were sent to nine "nations" of the confederacy.† From this time the chiefs of the Tuteloes, as well as of the Nanticokes and the Delawares, took their seats in the Council of the League, a position which they still hold in the Canadian branch of the confederacy, though the tribes whom they represent have ceased to exist as such, and have become absorbed in the larger nations.

It would seem, however, that their removal from their lands on the Susquehanna to the proper territory of the Six Nations did not take place immediately after their reception into the League, and perhaps was never wholly completed. In an "account of the location of the Indian tribes," prepared by Sir William Johnson in November, 1768, the four small tribes of "Nanticokes, Conoys, Tutecoes [an evident misprint] and Saponeys," are bracketed together in the list as mustering in all two hundred men, and are described as "a people removed from the southward and settled on or about the Susquehanna, on lands allotted by the Six Nations."‡

---

* N.Y. Hist. Col. Vol. vi, p. 811.
† Stone's Life of Sir William Johnson, Vol. i, p. 484.
‡ *Ibid.*, Vol. ii, p. 487.

Though the Tuteloes were thus recognized as one of the nations of the confederacy, and as such kept up their distinct tribal organization they were regarded as being in a special manner the friends and allies of the Cayugas. The latter, a tribe always noted for their kindly temper, received the new comers within their territory, and gave them a site for their town, which of course brought with it the hunting and fishing privileges necessary for their existence. The principal Cayuga villages were clustered about the lake to which the nation has given its name. South of them lay the land assigned to the Tuteloes. Their chief settlement, according to a careful observer, was on the east side of Cayuga inlet, about three miles from the south end of Cayuga lake, and two miles south of Ithaca. "The town was on the high ground south of the school-house, nearly opposite Buttermilk Falls, on the farm of James Fleming. On the Guy Johnson's map of 1771, it figures (by a slight misprint) as Todevigh-rono. It was called in the Journal of General Dearborn, Coreorgonel; In the Journal of George Grant (1779), Dehoriss-kanadia; and on a map made about the same date Kayeghtalagealat."*

The town was destroyed in 1779 by General Sullivan, in the expedition which avenged, so disastrously for the Six Nations, the ravages committed by them upon the settlements of their white neighbors. The result, as is well known, was the destruction of the ancient confederacy. Of the broken tribes, some fragments remained in their

---

* I am indebted for this and much other valuable information to my friend General John S. Clark, of Auburn, N.Y., who has made the location and migrations of the Indian tribes the subject of a special study. Of the above names Dehoriss kanadia is apparently a corruption of the Mohawk words *Tehoterigh kanada*, Tutelo town. The other words are probably, like most Indian names of places, descriptive designations, but are too much corrupted to be satisfactorily deciphered.

original seats, submitting to the conquerors. All the Mohawks, the greater part of the Cayugas, about half of the Onondagas, and many of the Oneidas, with a few of the Senecas and Tuscaroras, followed Brant to Canada. The British government furnished them with lands, mostly along the Grand River, in the territory which in ancient times had been conquered by the Iroquois from the people who were styled the Neutral Nation. The Tuteloes accompanied their friends the Cayugas. A place was found for them in a locality which seemed at the time attractive and desirable, but which proved most unfortunate for them. They built their town on a pleasant elevation, which stretches along the western bank of the Grand River, and still bears the name of Tutelo Heights. Under this name it now forms a suburb of the city of Brantford.

Fifty years ago, when the present city was a mere hamlet, occupied by a few venturous Indian traders and pioneers, the Tutelo cabins were scattered over these heights, having in the midst their "long-house" in which their tribal councils were held, and their festivals celebrated. They are said to have numbered then about two hundred souls. They retained apparently the reckless habits and love of enjoyment which had distinguished them in former times. Old people still remember the uproar of the dances which enlivened their council-house. Unhappily, the position of their town brought them into direct contact with the white settlements. Their frames, enfeebled by dissipation, were an easy prey to the diseases which followed in the track of the new population. In 1882, the Asiatic cholera found many victims on the

Indian Reserve. The Tuteloes, in proportion to their numbers, suffered the most. The greater part of the tribe perished. Those who escaped clung to their habitations a few years longer. But the second visitation of the dreadful plague in 1848 completed the work of the first. The Tutelo nation ceased to exist. The few survivors fled from the Heights to which they have left their name, and took refuge among their Cayuga friends. By intermarriage with these allies, the small remnant was soon absorbed; and in the year 1870, only one Tutelo of the full blood was known to be living, the last survivor of the tribe of stalwart hunters and daring warriors whom Lawson encountered in Carolina a hundred and seventy years before.

This last surviving Tutelo lived among the Cayugas, and was known to them by the name of Nikonha. Okonha in the Cayuga dialect signifies mosquito. Nikonha was sometimes, in answer to my inquiries rendered "mosquito," and sometimes "little," perhaps in the sense of mosquito-like. His Tutelo name was said to be Waskiteng; its meaning could not be ascertained, and it was perhaps merely a corruption of the English word mosquito. At all events, it was by the rather odd cognomen of "Old Mosquito," that he was commonly known among the whites; and he was even so designated, I believe, in the pension list, in which he had a place as having served in the war of 1812. What in common repute was deemed to be the most notable fact in regard to him was his great age. He was considered by far the oldest man on the Reserve. His age was said to exceed a century; and in confirmation of this opinion it was related that he had fought under Brant in the American war of Independence. My friend, Chief George Johnson, the government interpreter, accompanied us to the residence of the old man, a log cabin, built on a small eminence near the centre of the Reserve. His appearance, as we first saw him, basking in the sunshine on the slope before his cabin, confirmed the reports which I had heard, both of his great age and of his marked intelligence. "A wrinkled, smiling countenance, a high forehead, half-shut eyes, white hair, a scanty, stubbly beard, fingers bent with age like a bird's claws," is the description recorded in my note-book. Not only in physiognomy, but also in demeanor and character, he differed strikingly from the grave and composed Iroquois among whom he dwelt. The lively, mirthful disposition of his race survived in full force in its latest member. His replies to our inquiries were intermingled with many jocose remarks, and much good-humored laughter.

He was married to a Cayuga wife, and for many years had spoken only the language of her people. But he had not forgotten his proper speech, and readily gave us the Tutelo renderings of nearly a hundred words. At that time my only knowledge of the Tuteloes had been derived frem the few notices comprised in Gallatin's Synopsis of the Indian Tribes, where they are classed with the nations of the Huron-Iroquois stock. At the same time, the distinguished author, with the scientific caution which marked all his writings, is careful to mention that no vocabulary of the language was known. That which now obtained showed, beyond question, that the language was totally distinct from the Huron-Iroquois tongues, and that it was closely allied to the languages of the Dacotan family.

The discovery of a tribe of Dakota lineage near the Atlantic coast was so unexpected and surprising that at first it was natural to suspect some mistake. The idea occurred that the old Tutelo might have been a Sioux captive, taken in the wars which were anciently waged between the Iroquois and the tribes of the far West. With the view of determining this point, I took the first opportunity, on my next visit to the Reserve, in October, 1870, of questioning the old man about his early history, and that of his people. His answers soon removed all doubt. He believed himself to be a hundred and six years old; and if so, his earliest recollections would go back to a time preceding by some years the Revolutionary war. At that time his people, the Tuteloes, were living in the neighborhood of two other tribes, the Saponies and the Patshenins or Botshenins. In the latter we may perhaps recognize the Ochineeches, whom Governor Spotteswood, in 1702, enumerated with the Saponies, Toteroes, and two other tribes, under the general name of Christanna Indians. The Saponies and Tuteloes, old Nikonha said, could understand one another's speech. About the language of the Patshenins, I neglected to inquire, but they were mentioned with the Saponies as a companion tribe. When the Tuteloes came to Canada with Brant, they parted with the Saponies at Niagara Falls, and he did not know what had become of them. His father's name was Onusowa; he was a chief among the Tuteloes. His mother (who was also a Tutelo), died when he was young, and he was brought up by an uncle. He had heard from old men that the Tuteloes formerly lived on a great river beyond Washington, which city he knew by that name. In early times they were a large tribe, but had wasted away through fighting. Their war parties used to go out frequently against various enemies. The tribes they most commonly fought with were the Tuscaroras, Senecas, and Cayugas. Afterwards his tribe came to Niagara (as he expressed it), and joined the Six Nations. He knew of no Tutelo of the full blood now living, except himself.

This, with some additions to my vocabulary, was the last information which I received from old Waskiteng, or Nikonha. He died a few months later (on the 21st of February, 1871), before I had an opportunity of again visiting the Reserve. There are, however, several half-castes, children of Tutelo mothers by Iroquois fathers, who know the language, and by the native law (which traces descent through the female) are held to be Tuteloes. One of them, who sat in the council as the representative of the tribe, and who, with a conservatism worthy of the days of old Sarum, was allowed to retain his seat after his constituency had disappeared, was accustomed to amuse his grave fellow-senators occasionally by asserting the right which each councillor possesses of addressing the council in the language of his people,—his speech, if necessity requires, being translated by an interpreter. In the case of the Tutelo chief the jest, which was duly appreciated, lay in the fact that the interpreters were dumfounded, and that the eloquence uttered in an unknown tongue had to go without reply.

From this chief, and from his aunt, an elderly dame, whose daughter was the wife of a leading Onondaga chief, I received a sufficient number of words and phrases of the language to give a good idea of its grammatical framework. Fortunately, the list of words obtained from the old Tutelo was extensive enough to afford a test of the correctness of the additional information thus procured. The vocabulary and the outlines of grammar which have been derived from these sources may, therefore, as far as they extend, be accepted as affording an authentic representation of this very interesting speech.

There is still, it should be added, some uncertainty in regard to the tribal name. So far as can be learned, the word Tutelo or Totero (which in the Iroquois dialects is variously pronounced Tiūterih or Tehōtirigh, Tehūtili, Tiūtei and Tūtie) has no meaning either in the Tutelo or the Iroquois language. It may have been originally a mere local designation, which has accompanied the tribe, as such names sometimes do, in its subsequent migrations. Both of my semi-Tutelo informants assured me that the proper national name — or the name by which the people were designated among themselves — was Yesáng or Yesáh, the last syllable having a faint nasal sound, which was sometimes barely audible. In this word we probably see the origin of the name, Nahyssan, applied by Lederer to the tribes of this stock. John Lederer was a German traveler who in May, 1670 — a year before Captain Batt's expedition to the Alleghenies — undertook, at the charge of the colonial government, an exploring journey in the same direction, though not with equal success. He made, however, some interesting discoveries. Starting from the Falls of the James river, he came, after twenty days of travel, to "Sapon, a village of the Nahyssans," situate on

27

a branch of the Roanoke river. These were, undoubtedly, the Saponas whom Captain Batt visited in the following year, the kindred and allies of the Tuteloes. Fifty miles beyond Sapon he arrived at Akenatzy, an island in the same river. "The island," he says, "though small, maintains many inhabitants, who are fixed in great security, being naturally fortified with fastnesses of mountains and water on every side,"* In these Akenatzies we undoubtedly see the Aconechos of Lawson, and the Ochineeches mentioned by Governor Spotteswood. Dr. Brinton, in his well-known work on the "Myths of the New World," has pointed out, also, their identity with the Occaneeches mentioned by Beverley in his "History of Virginia," and in doing so has drawn attention to the very interesting facts recorded by Beverley respecting their language.†

According to this historian, the tribes of Virginia spoke languages differing so widely that natives "at a moderate distance" apart did not understand one another. They had, however, a "general language," which people of different tribes used in their intercourse with one another, precisely as the Indians of the north, according to La Hontan, used the "Algonkine," and as Latin was employed in most parts of Europe, and the Lingua Franca in the Levant. These are Beverley's illustrations. He then adds the remarkable statement: "The general language here used is that of the Occaneeches, though they have been but a small nation ever since these parts were known to the English; but in what their language may differ from

---

* See "The Discoveries of John Lederer," reprinted by O. H. Harpel. Cincinnati, 1879, p. 17.
† See the note on page 309 of Dr Brinton's volume, 2d edition.

that of the Algonkins I am not able to determine."†
Further on he gives us the still more surprising information that this "general language" was used by the "priests
and coniurors" of the different Virginian nations in performing their religious ceremonies, in the same manner
(he observes) "as the Catholics of all nations do their
Mass in the Latin."‡

The Akenatzies or Occaneeches would seem to have
been, in some respects, the chief or leading community
among the tribes of Dakotan stock who formerly inhabited Virginia. That these tribes had at one time a large and
widespread population may be inferred from the simple
fact that their language, like that of the widely scattered
Algonkins (or Ojibways) in the northwest, became the
general medium of communication for the people of different nationalities in their neighborhood. That they had
some ceremonial observances (or, as Beverley terms
them, "adorations and conjurations") of a peculiar and
impressive cast, like those of the western Dakotas, seems
evident from the circumstance that the intrusive tribes
adopted this language. and probably with it some of these
observances, in performing their own religious rites. We
thus have a strong and unexpected confirmation of the
tradition prevailing among the tribes both of the Algonkin
and of the Iroquois stocks, which represents them as coming originally from the far north, and gradually over-
spreading the country on both sides of the Alleghanies,
from the Great Lakes to the mountain fastnesses of the
Cherokees. They found, it would seem, Virginia, and pos-

† History of Virginia (1st edition), p.161.
‡ *Ibid.*, p.171.

sibly the whole country east of the Alleghenies, from the Great Lakes to South Carolina, occupied by tribes speaking languages of the Dakotan stock. That the displacement of these tribes was a very gradual process, and that the relations between the natives and the encroaching tribes were not always hostile, may be inferred not only from the adoption of the aboriginal speech as the general means of intercourse, but also from the terms or amity on which these tribes of diverse origin, native and intrusive, were found by the English to be living together.

That the Tutelo tongue represents this "general language" of which Beverley speaks—this aboriginal Latin of Virginia—cannot be doubted. It may, therefore be deemed a language of no small historical importance. The fact that this language, which was first obscurely heard of in Virginia two hundred years ago, has been brought to light in our day on a far-off Reservation in Canada, and there learned from the lips of the latest surviving member of this ancient community, must certainly be considered one of the most singular occurrences in the history of science.

Apart from the mere historical interest of the language, its scientific value in American ethnology entitles it to a careful study. As has been already said, a comparison of its grammar and vocabulary with those of the western Dakota tongues has led to the inference that the Tutelo language was the older form of this common speech. This conclusion was briefly set forth in some remarks which I had the honor of addressing to this Society at the meeting of December 19, 1879, and is recorded in the published minutes of the meeting. Some years afterwards, and after the earlier portion of this essay was written, I had the pleasure, at the meeting of the American Association for the Advancement of Science, held in Montreal, in September, 1882, of learning from my friend, the Rev. J. Owen Dorsey, of the Smithsonian Institution, who has resided for several years as a missionary among the western Dakotas, and has made careful researches into their languages and history, that they have a distinct tradition that their ancestors formerly dwelt east of the Mississippi. In fact, the more southern Dakotas declare their tribes to be offshoots of the Winnebagoes, who till recently resided near the western shore of Lake Michigan. A comparison of their dialects, made with Mr. Dorsey's aid, fully sustains this assertion. Mere traditionary evidence, as is well known, cannot always be relied on; but when it corresponds with conclusions previously drawn from linguistic evidence, it has a weight which renders it a valuable confirmation.

The portrait of old Nikonha, an accurate photograph, will serve to show, better than any description could do, the characteristics of race which distinguished his people. The full oval outline of face, and the large features of almost European cast, were evidently not individual or family traits, as they reappear in the Tutelo half-breeds on the Reserve, who do not claim a near relationship to Nikonha. Those who are familiar with the Dakotan physiognomy will probably discover a resemblance of type between this last representative of the Virginian Tutelos and their congeners, the Sioux and Mandans of the western plains.

31

THE TUTELO LANGUAGE.

In the following outline of Tutelo grammar, it has been deemed advisable to bring its forms into comparison with those of the western languages of the same stock. For this purpose the Dakota and Hidatsa (or Minnetaree) languages were necessarily selected, being the only tongues of this family of which any complete account has yet been published. For the information respecting these languages I am indebted to the Dakota Grammar and Dictionary of the Rev. S. R. Riggs (published in the Smithsonian Contributions to Knowledge) and the Hidatsa Grammar and Dictionary of Dr. Washington Matthews (published in Dr. Shea's Library of American Linguistics), both of them excellent works, of the highest scientific value.

The Alphabet.

The alphabetical method which has been followed by me in writing this language, as well as the Iroquois dialects, is based on the well-known system proposed by the Hon. John Pickering, and generally followed by American missionaries, whose experience has attested its value. The modifications suggested for the Indian languages by Professor Whitney and Major Powell have been adopted, with a few exceptions, which are due chiefly to a desire to employ no characters that are not found in any well-furnished printing-office.

The letters *b*, *d*, *h*, *k*, *l*, *m*, *n*, *p*, *s*, *t*, *w*, *y*, *z* are sounded as in English, the *s* having always its sharp sound, as in *mason*. The vowels are sounded generally as in Italian or German, with some modifications expressed by diacritical marks, thus:

a, as in *father*; in accented syllables written *ā*.
ă, like the German *a* in *Mann*.
ä, like *a* in *mat*.
â, like *a* in *fall*.
e, like *a* in *fate*; in accented syllables *ē*.
ě, like *e* in *met*.
i, like *i* in *machine*; in accented syllables *ī*.
ĭ, like *i* in *pin*.
o, as in *note* ; in accented syllables *ō*.
ŏ; like the French *o* in *bonne*.
ò, like *o* in *not*.
ú, as in *rule*, or like *oo* in *pool*; in accented syllables *ū*.
ŭ, like *u* in *pull*.
ù, like *u* in *but*; in an accented syllable written *û*.
ü, like the French *u* in *dur*.

The diphthongs are, *ai*, like our long *i* in *pine*; *au*, like *ou* in *loud*; *âi*, like *oi* in *boil*; *iu*, like *u* in *pure*.

The consonants requiring special notice are :

ç, like *sh* in *shine*.
g, always hard, as in *go*, *get*, *give*.
j, like *z* in *azure*.
ñ, like the French nasal *n* in *an*, *bon*, *un*.
q, like the German *ch* in *Loch*, or the Spanish *j* in *joven*

The sound of the English *ch* in *chest* is represented by *tç*; the *j* and *dg* in *judge* by *dj*.

The apostrophe (') indicates a slight hiatus in the pronounciation of a word, which is often, though not always, caused by the dropping of a consonantal sound.

In general, the diacritical marks over the vowels are omitted, except in the accented syllable—that is, the syllable on which the stress of voice falls. It is understood that when a vowel (other than the *ù*) has a mark of any kind over it, the syllable in which it occurs is the accented or emphatic syllable of the word. Experience shows that the variations in the sound of a vowel in unaccented syllables, within the limits represented by the foregoing alphabet, are rarely of sufficient importance to require to be noted in taking down a new language. The only exception is in the sound marked *ù*, which occasionally has to be indicated in unaccented syllables, to distinguish it from the *u*, with which it has no similarity of sound. It is, in fact, more frequently a variation of the *a* than of any other vowel sound.

Occasionally the accented syllable is indicated by an acute accent over the vowel. This method is adopted principally when the vowel has a brief or obscure sound, as in *misáñi*, I alone, which is pronounced in a manner midway between *misāñi* and *misùñi*.

Phonology.

The Tutelo has the ordinary vowel sounds, but the distinction between *e* and *i*, and between *o* and *u* is not

34

always clear. The word for "mother" was at one time written *henā*, and at another *ina*; the word for "he steals" was heard as *manōma* and *manūma*. In general, however, the difference of these vowels was sufficiently apparent. The obscure sound of *ù* (or in accented syllables *û*) was often heard, but when the word in which it occurred was more distinctly uttered, this sound was frequently developed into a clearer vowel. Thus *hùstōi*, arm, became *histō*; *mùstē*, spring (the season), became *mastē*; *asûñi*, white. became *asāñi*; or (losing the nasal sound) *asāi*, and so on. The use of the character *ù* (or *û*) in this language could probably be dispensed with.

The consonantal sounds which were heard were: *p* (or *b*), *t* (or *d*), *k* (or *g*), *h* (and *q*), *l*, *m*, *n*, *s*, *w*, and *y*, and the nasal *ñ*. Neither *f*, *v*, nor *r* was heard, and *ç* (*sh*) only as a variant of *s*. Harsh combinations of consonants were rare. The harshest was that of *tsk*, as in *wagutska*, child, and this was not frequent.* Words usually end in a vowel or a liquid. A double consonant at the commencement of a word is rare. It perhaps only occurs in the combination *tç* (*tsh*) and in contractions, as *ksāñkai*, nine, for *kasāñkai*.

It is doubtful if the sonants *b*, *d* and *g* occur, except as variants of the surd consonants *p*, *t* and *k*; yet in certain words sonants were pretty constantly used. Thus in the pronouns *miñgītowe*, mine, *yiñgītowe*, thine, *iñgītowe*, his, the *g* was almost always sounded.

The *l* and *n* were occasionally interchanged, as in *lāni*

---

* In *wagutska* (Dakota, *koçka*), *suntka*, younger brother (Dak., *sunka*); *tçoñgo* or *tçuñki*, dog (Dak., *cuñka*) and many similar words, the *t* is apparently an adscititious sound, inserted by a mere trick of pronunciation. The Hidatsa carries this practice further, and constantly introduces the sound oft before the sharp *s*. The Tutelo *isi*, foot, becomes *itsi* in Hidatsa; *sanī*, cold, becomes *tsinia*, &c

and *nāni*, three, *letçi* and *netçi*, tongue. In general, however, the two elements seemed to be distinct. The aspirate was somewhat stronger than the English *h*, and frequently assumed the force of the German *ch* or the Spanish *j* (represented in our alphabet by *q*). Whether there were really two distinct sounds or not, could not be positively ascertained. The same word was written at one time with *h*, and at another with *q*.

The nasal *ñ* is properly a modification of the preceding vowel, and would have been more adequately rendered by a mark above or below the vowel itself; but it has seemed desirable to avoid the multiplication of such diacritical marks. This nasal is not to be confounded with the sound of *ng* in *ring*, which is a distinct consonantal element, and in the Polynesian dialects often commences a word. In the Tutelo this latter sound only occurs before a *k* or hard *g*, and is then represented by *ñ*. It is, in fact, in this position, merely the French nasal sound, modified by the palatal consonant. The nasal *ñ* is also modified by the labials *b* and *p*, before which it assumes the sound of *m*. Thus the Tutelo word for day, *nahāmbi*, or (in the construct form) *nahāmp*, is properly a modification of *nahāñbi* or *nahāñp*. In all words in which it occurs, the nasal sound was at times very faintly heard, and was occasionally so little audible that it was not noted, while at other times an *n* was heard in its place. The word for knife was written at different times *masĕñi* and *masāi*; that for sky, *matōñi*, *matōi*, *mantōi*, and *mañtoi*; that for day, *nahāmbi*, *nahāmp*, *nahāñp*, and *nahāp*; that for winter, *wānē*, *wānéñi*, and *wanēi*; that for one, *nōs* and *noñs*,

36

and so on. Whether this indistinctness of the nasal sound belongs to the language, or was a peculiarity of the individuals from whom the speech was learned, could not be satisfactorily determined.

The tendency of the language, as has been said, is to terminate every word with a vowel sound. When a monosyllable or dissyllable ends with a consonant, it is usually in a construct form, and is followed by another word grammatically related to it. Thus, *hisépi*, axe, *hisēp miñgitowe*, my axe; *monti*, a bear, *mont nosā*, one bear ; *tçòñgo* (or *tçònki*), dog, *tçònk epīsel*, good dog; *nahāmbi*, day, *nahāmp lāni*, three days.

The following brief comparative list, extracted from the more extensive vocabulary hereafter given, will show the forms which similar words take in the allied dialects, Tutelo, Dakota (or Sioux proper) and Hidatsa (or Minnetaree) :

Tutelo.	Dakota.	Hidatsa.	
āti	*ate*	*ati*	father
inā, henā, henûñ	*ina*	*hinu, hu, ikùs*	mother
tāgūtçkai	*takoçku, tçiñkçi*	*idiçi*	son
suntka	*suñka*	*tsuka*	younger brother
īh, ihī	*i*	*i*	mouth
nētçi, nētsi, lētçi	*tçeji*	*neji*	tongue
ihī	*hi*	*i, isa, hi*	tooth
lōti	*dote*	*doti, loti*	throat
isī	*siha*	*itsi*	foot
wasūt	*nasu*	*tsuata*	brain
wāyī, wayīi	*we*	*idi*	blood
atī	*tipi*	*ati*	house
maséñi, masāi	*isañ, miñna*	*maetsi*	knife
mī	*wi*	*midi*	sun (or moon)
nihāmpi, nihāñpi	*añpetu*	*mape*	day

37

manī	mini	mini	water
amāñi amāi	maka	ama	land
tcūñki, tçoñgo	çunka	maçuka	dog
wānéñi, wānēi	wani	mana	winter
tañi	ptañ	mata,	autumn
asáñi, asāi, aséi	sañ	atùki, ohùki	white
asépi	sapa	çipi	black
sīi wāsi	zi	tsi, tsidi	yellow
tē	ta	te	dead
sani	sni	tsinia	cold
nosāi, noñç	wantça, wantçi	nuéts, luétsa	one
nombāi	noñpa	nopa	two
nāni lāni	yamni	dámi, lawi	three
topai	topa	topa	four
kisāhai	zaptañ	kihu	five
akáspe	çakpe	akama, akawa	six
sāgomink	çakowiñ	sapua	seven
luta	yuta, wota	duti	to eat
howa	u, uwa	hu	to come
kitci	watçi	kidiçi	to dance
mahanañka	yañka, nañka	naka	to sit, remain
ktéwa, kitésel	kte	kitahé	to kill

It must be borne in mind that the sounds of *m*, *b*, and *w* are interchangeable in the Hidatsa, and that *d*, *l*, *n*, and *r* are also interchangeable. A similar confusion or interchange of these elements is to some extent apparent in the Dakota and the Tutelo languages. Taking this fact into consideration, the similarity or rather identity of such words as *mi* in Tutelo and *wi* in Dakota, meaning "sun," and *loti* in Tutelo, *dote* in Dakota, and *dote* or *lote* in Hidatsa, meaning "brain," becomes apparent.

The nasal sounds, which are so common in the Dakota and the Tutelo are wanting in the Hidatsa, while the *s* of the two former languages frequently becomes *ts* in Hidatsa. These dialectical peculiarities explain the difference between the words for younger brother, *suntka*, Tu., *suñka*, Da., *tsuka*, Hi., between *isi*, foot, Tu., and *itsi*, Hi., between *maseñi*, knife, Tu., and *maetsi*, Hi. It will be noticed that the words in Tutelo are frequently longer and fuller in sound than the corresponding words in the other languages, as though they were nearer the original forms from which the words in the various Dakota tongues were derived.

As is usually the case with allied tongues, the grammatical resemblances of the languages of this stock are much more striking and instructive than those which appear in the mere comparison of isolated words.

Substantives and Adjectives.

The Tutelo, like the Dakota and the Hidatsa, has no inflection of the substantive to indicate the plural number; but in both the Tutelo and the Dakota, the plural of adjectives is frequently expressed by what may be termed a natural inflection, namely, by a reduplication. In the Dakota, according to Mr. Riggs, the initial syllable is sometimes reduplicated, as *ksapa*, wise, pl. *ksaksapa*; *tañka*, great, pl. *tañktañka*; sometimes it is the last syllable, as *waçté*, good, pl. *waçtéçte*; and occasionally it is a middle syllable, as, *tañkiñyañ*, great, pl. *tañkiñkiñyañ*.

Sometimes the adjective in Dakota takes the suffix *pi*, which makes the plural form of the verb, as *waçte*; good *witçasta waçtépi*, good men, i. e., they are good men.

39

Similar forms exist in the Tutelo. The adjective, or some part of it, is reduplicated in the plural, and at the same time a verbal suffix is frequently if not always added, thus ; *ati api*, good house, pl. *ati apipisel*, good houses (those are good houses); *ati itáñi*, large house, pl. *ati itañtáñsel*; *ati okayēke*, bad house, pl. *ati okayeyēkesel*; *ati asáñ*, white house, pl. *ati asañsáñsel*. Occasionally the reduplication takes a peculiar form, as in *ati kutska*, small house. pl. *ati kotskutskaisel*. In one instance the plural differs totally from the singular ; *ati sui*, long house, pl. *ati yumpañkatskaisel*.

The plural verbal termination is frequently used without the reduplication ; as, *wahtáke bi* (or *pi*), good man, *wahtáke biwa* (or *bise*), he is a good man ; pl. *wahtáke bīhla* (or *bihlése*), they are good men. So *tçoñge bise*, good dog (or, it is a good dog), pl. *tcoñge bihlése*.

The plural form by reduplication does not appear to exist in the Hidatsa.

The Rev. J. Owen Dorsey, who has made a special study of the western Dakota languages, finds in the Omaha (or Dhegiha) dialect a peculiar meaning given to this reduplicate plural of adjectives. The following examples will illustrate this signification. *Jiñgā*, small, becomes in the reduplicate form *jiñjiñga*, which refers to small objects of different kinds or sizes. *Sagī*, firm, fast, hard, makes *sāsagi* or *sagīgi*, which is employed as in the following example : *wēdhihide sagīgihnan kañbdha*, I wish tools that are hard, and of different kinds, them only. Here the suffix *hnān* expresses the meaning of "only;" the reduplication of the adjective gives the sense expressed by the words "of different kinds." *Sābe*, black, makes *sāsabe*, black here and there. *Gdhejē*, spotted, becomes *gdhejāja* spotted in many places. *Pīaji*, bad, makes *pīpiaji*, as in *uçkañ pipiaji*, different bad deeds. *Nūjiñga* (apparently a compound or derivative form, from *jiñgā*, small), means "boy," *i. e.*, small man; *nūjiñjīñga*, boys of different sizes and ages.* It would seem from these examples that in this language the reduplication expresses primarily the idea of variety, from which that of plurality in many cases follows. This meaning is not indicated by Mr. Riggs in his Dakota grammar, and it was not detected by me in the Tutelo, but it is not impossible that it actually exists in both languages. It is deserving of notice that while no inflection of the noun is found in the Iroquois to express plurality, this meaning is indicated in the adjective by the addition of *s*, or *hoñs*, affixed to the adjective when it is combined with the noun. Thus from *kanóñsa*, house, and *wīyo*, handsome, we have *konoñsīyo*, handsome house, pl. *kanoñsīyos*, handsome houses. So *kareñnaksen*, bad song, pl. *kareñnaksens*, bad songs; *kanākares*, long pole, pl. *kanakarēshoñs*, long poles.

It is also remarkable that the peculiar mode of forming the plural, both of substantives and of adjectives, by reduplication of the first syllable or portion of the word, is found in several Indian languages spoken west of the Rocky Mountains, and belonging to families entirely distinct from one another, and from the Dakota. Thus in the

---

* I am indebted to Mr. Dorsey's letters for this and much other information of great interest respecting the western languages of the Dakota stock, forming part of his extensive work. which we may hope will soon be published.

41

Selish language we have *lùáus*, father, pl. *lùlùáus*; *tána*, ear, pl. *tùntána*; *skùltamíqo*, man, pl. *skùlkùltamiqo*; *qáest*, good, pl. *qùsqáest*. In the Sahaptin, *pītin*, girl, pl. *pipítin*; *tāhs*, good, pl. *titāhs*. In the Kizh language, *woróit*, man, pl. *wororōt*; *tçinni*, small, pl. *tçitçinni*.† This has been termed, and certainly seems, a natural mode of forming the plural. It is therefore somewhat surprising to find it restricted in America to a comparatively small group of linguistic families. It is still more noteworthy that in the Polynesian dialects, which in their general characteristics differ so widely from the Indian languages, this same method of forming the plural is found, but confined, as in the Dakota tongues, to the adjective; thus we have *laau tele*, large tree, pl. *laau tetele*, large trees; *taata maitai*, good man, pl. *taata maitatai*, good men; *mahaki*, sick, pl. *mahamahaki*, sick (persons).‡ This is a subject in linguistic science which merits farther investigation.

Numerals.

The near resemblance of the first seven numerals in the Tutelo, Dakota, and Hidatsa is sufficiently shown in the vocabulary. The manner in which the compound numbers are formed is also similar in the three languages. In the Dakota *ake*, again, is prefixed to the simple numerals to form the numbers above ten, as *ake wañjidañ*, eleven ; *ake noñpa*, twelve. In the Tutelo the same word (usually

† Ethnography and Philology of the U.S. Exploring Expedition under Chas. Wilkes, pp. 534, et seq.
‡ Ibid., p. 244

softened to *age*) is used, as *agenōsai*, eleven; *agenombai*, twelve. In the Hidatsa *aqpi* (or *ahpi*), signifying a part or division, is employed, as *aqpi-duetsa*, eleven; *aqpi-dopa*, twelve.

In Dakota, *wiktçemna*, ten, and *noñpa*, two, form *wiktçemna noñpa*, twenty. In Tutelo the form is the same; *putçka nomba*, tens-two. In Hidatsa it is similar, but the position of the words is reversed, twenty being *dopá-pitika*, two tens.

The ordinal numbers, after the first, are formed in all three languages by prefixing *i* or *ei* to the cardinal numbers, as in Dakota, *inoñpa*, second ; *iyamni*, third ; *itopa*, fourth. In Hidatsa, *idopa*, second ; *idani*, third ; *itopa*, fourth. In Tutelo I received *einombai*, twice; *eināni* thrice; *eintōpai*, four times. This rendering was given by the interpreter, but the true meaning was probably the same as in the Dakota and Hidatsa. The word for "first" is peculiar in all three languages; in Dakota, *tokaheya*, in Hidatsa, *itsika*, in Tutelo, *etāhni*.

In the Tutelo the numerals appear to have different forms; or perhaps, more accurately speaking, different terminations, according to the context in which they are used. The following are examples of these forms, the first or abridged form being apparently used in ordinary counting, and the others when the numerals are employed in conjunction with other words. The various pronunciations of my different informants—and sometimes of the same informant at different times—are also shown in these examples.

43

Separate.	Construct.	Variations.
1 *nōñs, nōs*	*nosāi, noñsāi*	*noséñ, nuseñ, noñsai, noñsa, nōsāñ, nōsāh, noñsah*
2 *nomp*	*nombāi*	*numbāi, nomba, nūmba, noñmbai, noñpa, nōmbāh, nombaq*
3 *lāt, nān*	*nāni*	*lāni, lānih, lāniq*
4 *tōp*	*topāi*	*toba, topah*
5 *kisē, kisáñ*	*kisāhai*	*kisāháñi*
6 *agās* or *akás,* *akāsp* }	*akáspē*	*akaspé, akāspei, agespeq*
7 *sāgóm*	*sagomēi*	*sagōmi, sāgōmiq, sagomiñk*
8 *pālán*	*palāni*	*palāniq*
9 *sā* or *sāñ, ksañk*	*ksāhkai*	*kasankai, ksākai*
10 *putçk, būtçk'*	*putskai*	*butçkai, putskáñi, putskāñ*
11 *āgenōsai*		*aginosai, akinosai*

Separate.	Construct Forms and Variations.
12 *agenomba*	*aginombai, akinombai*
13 *agelani*	*agilāli, akilāni*
14 *agetoba*	*akitōpa*
15 *agegīsai*	*akikisāhai*
16 *agegāspe*	*akikaspei*
17 *agesagōmi*	*akisagomei*
18 *agepalāni*	*akipalali*
19 *agekesañka*	*akikasañkai*
20 *putska nomba,* *putçka nombai* }	*putska nombai*
30 *putska nani*	*putçka lani*
40 *putska tobai*	
100 *ukenī nōsā*	*okenī*
1000 *ukenī putskai*	

The numeral follows the noun which it qualifies. If the noun terminates in a vowel not accented, the vowel is usually dropped, while the numeral assumes its constuctor or lengthened form, and is sometimes closed with a

44

strong aspirate. Thus, from *miháñi*, woman, we have *mihañ nosā* or *mihañ noñsāi*, one woman; *mihañ nombaq*, two women; *mihañ laniq*, three women, &c. From *tçoñgo* or *tçoñki*, dog, *tcoñk nosāh*, one dog; *tcoñk nombaq* two dogs. From *monti*, bear, *mont nōsāh*, one bear; *mont nombah*, two bears. From *nahambi*, day, *nahámp nosāh*, one day, *nahamp nombai*, two days; *nahamp lāniq*, three days, &c. It will be seen that the dropping of the final vowel of the noun has the effect of giving a sharper sound to the preceding consonant. When the final vowel is accented, no change takes place in the noun; thus *atī*, house; *atī noñsai*, one house; *atī noñbai*, two houses; *atī laniq*, three houses, &c.

No such difference between the simple and the construct forms of the numerals appears to exist either in the Dakota or in the Hidatsa. This is one evidence, among others, of the greater wealth of inflections which characterizes the Tutelo language.

Pronouns.

There are in the Tutelo, as in the Dakota, two classes of pronouns, the separate pronouns, and the affixed or incorporated pronouns. The former, however, are rarely used, except for the purpose of emphasis. In the Dakota the separate pronouns are *miye* or *miç*. I, *niye*, or *niç*, thou or ye, *iye*, or *iç*, he or they, and *uñkiye* or *uñkie*, we. In the Tutelo, *mīm* signifies I or we, *yīm*, thou or ye, *im*, he or they, which was sometimes lengthened to *imahēse*. A still more emphatic form is made with the termination *sái* or *sáñi*, giving the sense of "alone," or rather perhaps "self," for which meaning the Dakota employs the separate pronouns already given, while the Hidatsa has a special form ; thus :

Tutelo.	Dakota.	Hidatsa.	
misāi or misáñi	miye (miç)	miqki	I myself (or I alone)
yisāi, or yesáñi	niye (niç)	niqki	thou
esāi, isāi or isáñi	iye (iç)	iqki	he
maesāi or maesáñi	uñkiye (uñkiç)	midoki	we

The Dakota *uñkiye* is said to be properly a dual form. The Tutelo apparently, like the Hidatsa, has no dual.

The affixed or incorporated pronouns have in the Tutelo, as in the Dakota and Hidatsa, two forms, nominative and objective. These forms in the three languages are very similar :

Tutelo.	Dakota.	Hidatsa.	
Nominative.			
ma, wa	wa, we	ma	I
ya, ye	ya, ye	da (na)	thou
mae, mai, wae, wai, man, mañk,	uñ		we
Objective.			
mi, wi	ma, mi	mi	me
yi, hi	ni	di (ni)	thee
e, ei, i		i	him
mae, mai, wae, wai	uñ		us

The objective forms are also used in all these languages as possessive pronouns, and they are affixed as nominatives to neuter or adjective verbs, in the first and second persons. The third personal pronoun is not expressed in the verb, at least in the singular number. In the plural the Tutelo indicates this pronoun by an inflection, both in the nominative and the objective. Thus *hahēwa*, he says, *hahéhla*, they say ; *minēwa*, I see him, *minéhla*, I see them.

The Hidatsa makes no distinction between the singular and the plural of the possessive pronouns. *Mi* signifies both my and our, *di*, they and your, and *i*, his and their. The Dakota distinguishes the plural by adding the particle *pi* to the noun. The Tutelo adds *pui* to the noun in the second person, and sometimes *lei* or *kai* to the third. With nouns signifying relationship, the Dakota indicates the possessive pronoun of the third person by adding *ku* to the noun. The Tutelo sometimes adds *ka* or *kai* not only in this person, but in the first and third persons, as shown in the following example:

Dakota.	Tutelo.			
suñka	*súntka*		younger brother	
misuñka	*wisúntk*	my	"	"
yisuñka	*yisúntk*	thy	"	"
suñkaku	*esúntka* or *esúntkai*	his	"	"
uñkisuñkapi	*maisúñtkai*	our	"	"
nisuñkapi	*yisúñtkapui*	your	"	"
suñkapi	*eisúñtkai*	their	"	"

In the Tutelo an *e* is sometimes prefixed to the possessive pronouns, as in *ati*, house, which makes

ewāti	my house	*emānti*	our house
eyāti	thy "	*eyātipūi*	your "
eāti	his "	*eāti-lei*	their "

In this case the final vowel of the pronouns *wi* and *yi* is elided before the initial *a* of the noun. So in *minēwa*, I

47

see him, the vowel of the prefixed pronoun *ma*, I, is elided before the vowel of the verb *inēwa*, to see. Some other euphonic changes of the possessive pronoun in the Tutelo are shown in the following example :

Dakota.	Tutelo.		
pa	*pasūi,*	head	
mapa	*mimpasūi*	my	head
nipa	*yiñpasūi,*	thy	"
pa	*epasūi,*	his	"
uñpapi	*emañkpasūi,*	our	heads
nipapi	*eyiñkpasūpui*	your	"
papi	*epasūi-lei*	their	"

In Tutelo, *tāt'*, my father, is an anomalous form, used instead of *māt'*, or *emāt'*. With the other affixes the word becomes *yāt'* (or *itāti*), thy father, *eāt'*, his father (or their father), *emaāt'*, our father, *eyātpui*, your father.

A good example of the use of the prefixed personal pronouns in the Tutelo is shown in the word for son. There were slight differences in the forms received from two of my informants, as here given:

witéka	*witékai*	my son
yitēka	*yitékai*	thy son
etéka	*etékai*	his son
mañktéka	*emañktékai*	our son
yitékabūi	*yitékabūi*	your son
etéka	*etekahlēi*	their son

Minēk', my uncle (in Dakota *midekçi*) is thus varied : *Yinēk'*, thy uncle (Dak. *nídekçi*), *einēk'*, his uncle (Dak. *deçitku*), *emainek*, our uncle, *einēkpui*, your uncle, *einek'* or *einek'-lei*, their uncle.

In the word for brother, *iñginumbāi* (or *iñkinumbāi*), the possessive pronouns are inserted after the first syllable, and in this instance they are used in the nominative form :

iñwaginumbāi	my brother	*maiiñginumbāi*	our brother
iñyagnumbāi	thy brother	*iñyaginumbabūi*	your brother
ingiginumbāi	his brother	*iñgiginumbāi*	their brother

The Dakota and Hidatsa have lengthened forms of the personal pronouns to indicate property in things, or "transferable possession." These are in the former, *mita*, my, *nita*, thy, and *ta*, his, as *mita-oñspe*, my axe, *nita-çuñke*, thy dog. These pronouns are also used with *koda*, friend, and *kitçuna*, comrade. In Hidatsa *mata*, *dita* (for *nita*), and *ita*, are used in a similar manner. In the Tutelo the pronouns of this form occurred in a few examples, but only with certain words of personal connection or relations, in which their use seems to resemble that of the Dakota pronouns with the words meaning "comrade" and "friend." Thus we heard *witāmañki*, my husband, *yitāmañki*, thy husband, *etāmañki*, her husband. So *witāmiheñ*, my wife (*i.e.* my woman), *yitāmiheñ*, thy wife; and *witagūtçkāi*, my son, *i.e.* "my boy," from *wagūtçkāi*, boy (evidently the same word as the Dakota *koçka*, young man). In the latter example *witagūtçkāi*, apparently expresses a lower bond or sense of relationship than *witékai*, — not "my child," but "my boy," or "my youth," who may leave me and go elsewhere at any time.

In Tutelo the pronouns indicating property or "transferable possession" were commonly found in a separate and apparently compound form, following the noun, which was then sometimes (though not always) heard in the shortened or "construct" form. Thus with *hisēpi*, axe, we have :

hisēp' migītŏwi	(or *mikītowi*) my axe	*hisēp' mahgītowi*	our axe
hisēp' yiñgītowi	thy axe	*hisēp' iñgītombūi*	your axe
hisēp' gītowi	his axe	*hisēp' gitohnēi*	their axe

So *sās*, bed, has *sās miñgītowi*, my bed, *sas yingītowi*, thy bed, *sas gītowi*, his bed.

With *tçoñgo*, dog, we find a different form:

tçoñgo wahkímpi	my dog	*tçongo maokímpi* (or *mahkimpi*)	our dog
tçoñgo yahkímpi	thy dog	*tçongo yahkimpūi*	your dog
tçoñgo eohkimpi	his dog	*tçoñgo kímpena*	their dog

The first of these forms, *migītowi*, &c., is evidently the same that appears in the Dakota *mitawa*, mine, *witawa*, thine, *tawa*, his, *uñkitawa*, ours. The Hidatsa has similar forms, *matamae*, *ditamae*, and *itamae*, often pronounced *matawae*, *nitawae*, and *itawae*. Dr. Matthews regards them as compounds formed by prefixing the pronouns *mata*, *dita* (*nita*) and *ita* to the noun *mae* (or *wae*) signifying personal property, which seems a very probable explanation.

The form *wahkímpi* may be similarly explained. In Dakota *kipá* signifies, to keep for me, and *kipí*, to hold or contain. The sense of property or possession is apparently implied, and *tçongo wahkímpi* in Tutelo probably means "the dog my property," or "the dog I have."

The possessive pronouns are used by themselves in Tutelo in the following affirmative and negative forms :

mimigītōwi (or *mimigītowe*, or *mikītowi*)	mine, or, it is mine
yiñgītowi (*yingītowe, yiñkītowi*)	thine, or, it is thine
iñgītowi (*iñgītowe, iñkītowi*)	his, or, it is his
maqgitowi (or *mahgītowe*, or *mahkitowi*)	ours, or, it is ours
yingitombūi (or *yiñkitombui*)	yours, or, it is yours
gitoññēsel (or *kitoññesel*)	theirs, or it is theirs

Negative Form.

kimigītonañ (*kimikītonañ*)	it is not mine
kiñyigītonañ	it is not thine
kigītonañ	it is not his
kinaqgitonañ	it is not ours
kiñyigītombōnañ	it is not yours
kigītoqnēnañ	it is not theirs

The proper form of the first personal affirmative is doubtless *migītowi* (or *mikītowe*). In *mimigītowi* the first syllable is evidently from the separate pronoun *mīm*, I, used for emphasis. In the Dakota the forms *miye mitawa*, me, mine, *niye nitawa*, thee, thine, &c., are used for the same purpose.

The negative form is not found in either the Dakota or the Hidatsa, and may be regarded as another instance of the greater wealth of inflections possessed by the Tutelo.

The following are the interrogative demonstrative and indefinite pronouns in the Tutelo, so far as they were ascertained. The Dakota and Hidatsa are added for comparison:

Tutelo.	Dakota.	Hidatsa.	
ētowā, or *hetōa*	*tuwe*	*tape*	who?
ākeñ, kaka	*taku*	*tapa*	what?
ētuk	*tukte*	*to; tua*	which?
tokēnùñ	*tona; tonaka*	*tuami*	how many?
tewakītùnwā	*tuwetawa*	*tapeitamae*	whose (is it)?
nēke, or *nēikiñ; heiki*	*de*	*hidi; kini*	this
yukān; hēwa; enā	*he; ka*	*hido; hino*	that
ohōn, or *ohō*	*ota*	*ahu*	many
hōk, hūk, ōkahōk	*owasiñ; iyuqpa*	*etsa; qakaheta*	all

The general resemblance of most of these forms is
apparent. In the Tutelo for "whose?" which might have
been written *tewagītùñwa*, we see the affix of the possessive pronoun (*gītowe*) inflected to make an interrogative
form. The Dakota and Hidatsa use the affix (*tawa* and
tamae) without the inflection.

The Verb.

There are two very striking peculiarities in which the
Dakota and Hidatsa dialects differ from most, if not all,
Indian languages of other stocks. These are: firstly, the
manner in which the personal pronoun is incorporated
with the verb; and, secondly, the extreme paucity or
almost total absence of inflections of mood and tense. In
the first of these peculiarities the Tutelo resembles its
western congeners ; in the second it differs from them in
a marked degree—more widely even than the Latin verb
differs from the English. These two characteristics
require to be separately noted.

In most Indian languages the personal pronouns, both

of the subject and of the object, are in some measure either united with the verb or indicated by an inflection. The peculiarity which distinguishes the languages of the Dakotan stock is found in the variable position of these incorporated pronouns. They may be placed at the beginning, at the end, or between any two syllables of the verb. The position of the pronoun is not, however, arbitrary and dependent on the pleasure of the speaker. It appears to be fixed for each verb, according to certain rules. These rules, however, seem not yet to have been fully determined, and thus it happens that a Dakota dictionary must give the place of the pronoun in every verb, precisely as a Latin dictionary must give the perfect tense of every verb of the third conjugation. Thus, for example, in the Dakota proper, *kaçká*, to bind (or rather "he binds"), makes wa*káçka*, I bind, ya*kakça*, thou bindest; *manoñ*, he steals, makes *mawánoñ*, I steal, *mayánoñ*, thou stealest ; and *etçíñ*, he thinks, makes *etçáñ*mi, I think, *etçáñ*ni, thou thinkest, the suffixed pronouns receiving a peculiar form. In the Hidatsa, *kiděçi*, he loves, makes ma*kiděçi*, I love, da*kiděçi*, thou lovest ; *eke*, he knows, becomes *ema*ke, I know, and *eda*ke, thou knowest ; and *kitsahike*, he makes good, becomes *kitsahike*ma, I make good, and *kitsahike*-da, thou makest good. The Tutelo has the pronouns sometimes prefixed, and sometimes inserted ; no instances have been found in which they are suffixed, but it is by no means improbable that such cases may occur, as verbs of this class are not common in either of the former languages, and our examples of conjugated verbs in Tutelo are not very numerous. Among them are the following :

1. Verbs with prefixed pronouns:
   lakpése, he drinks
   ya*lakpése*, thou drinkest
   wa*lakpése*, I drink
   hiantkapēwa, he sleeps
   ya*hiantkapēwa*, thou sleepest
   wa*hiantkapēwa*, I sleep
   tēwa, he is dead
   yi*tēwa*, thou art dead
   wi*tēwa*, I am dead

2. The verbs in which the pronouns are inserted seem to be the most numerous class. The following are examples:
   hahēwa, he says
   *ha*yi*hēwa*, thou sayest
   *ha*wa*hēwa*, I say
   mahanáñka, he sits down
   *maha*yi*náñka*, then sittest down
   *maha*mi*náñka*, I sit down
   iñksēha, he laughs
   *iñya*k*sēha*, tliou lauglitst
   *iñwa*k*sēha*, I laugh
   ohảta, he sees
   *o*ya*hảta*, thou seest
   *o*wa*hảta*, I see

The pronouns may be thus inserted in a noun, used with a verbal sense. Thus *wahtāka* or *wahtakai*, man or Indian, may be conjugated:

54

wahtākai, he is an Indian
*wa*yih*tākai*, thou art an Indian
*wa*mih*tākai*, I am an Indian

It is remarkable, however, that the pronoun of the first person plural is usually (though not always) prefixed. Thus from *mahanáñka*, he sits down, we have (as above) *maha*mi*nañka*, I sit down, and mañk*mahanánka*, we sit down. So, ma*iñksēha* (or sometimes wa*iñksēha*), we laugh, and ma*ohata*, we see. On the other hand, we find *ha*mank*hewa*, we say, from *hahewa*, he says, making (as above) *hawahewa*, I say.

The word *manoñ*, he steals, has in Dakota the pronouns inserted, as is shown in the examples previously given. The similar word in Tutelo, *manōma* or *manūma*, has them prefixed, as y*imanōma*, thou stealest, ma*manōma*, I steal. But on one occasion this word was given in a different form, as *manundāñi*, he steals; and in this example the pronouns were inserted, the form of the first personal pronoun, and of the verb itself in that person, being at the same time varied, as ma*yinundāñi*, thou stealest, ma*minundame*, I steal. In Dakota the place of the pronoun is similarly varied by a change in the form of the verb. Thus *baksá*, to cut off with a knife, makes *ba*wà*ksa*, I cut off (with the pronoun inserted), while *kaksá*, to cut off with an axe, makes wa*káksa*, I cut off (with the pronoun prefixed), and so in other like instances.

The other peculiarity of the Dakota and Hidatsa languages, which has been referred to, viz., the paucity, or rather absence, of all changes of mood and tense which can properly be called inflections, is in striking contrast with the abundance of these changes which mark the Tutelo verb. The difference is important, especially as indicating that the Tutelo is the older form of speech. It is an established law in the science of linguistics that, in any family of languages, these which are of the oldest formation, or, in other words, which approach nearest to the mother speech, are the most highly inflected. The derivative or more recent tongues are distinguished by the comparative fewness of the grammatical changes in the vocables. The difference in this respect between the Tutelo and the western branches of this stock is so great that they seem to belong to different categories or genera in the classification of languages. The Tutelo may properly be styled an inflected language, while the Dakota, the Hidatsa, and apparently all the other western dialects of the stock, must be classed among agglutinated languages, the variations of person, number, mood and tense being denoted by affixed or inserted particles.

Thus in the Hidatsa there is no difference, in the present tense, between the singular and the plural of a verb. *Kidĕçi* signifies both "he loves" and "they love;" *makidĕçi*, "I love," and "we love." In the future a distinction is made in the first and second persons. *Dakidĕcidi* signifies "thou wilt love," of which *dakidĕcidiha* is the plural, "ye will love." In this language there is no mark of any kind, even by affixed particles, to distinguish the present tense from the past, nor even, in the third person, to distinguish the future from the other tenses. *Kidĕçi* signifies he loves, he loved, and he will love. The Dakota is a little better furnished in this way. The plural is distinguished from the singular by the addition of the particle *pi*, and in the first person by prefixing the pronoun *uñ*, they, in lieu of *wa* or *we*, I. Thus *kaçká*, he binds, becomes *kaçká*pi, they bind. *Wakaçka*, I bind, becomes uñ*kaçka*pi, we bind. No distinction is made between the present and the past tense. *Kaçká* is both he binds and he bound. The particle *kta*, which is not printed and apparently not pronounced as an affix, indicates the future. It sometimes produces a slight euphonic change in the final vowel of the verb. Thus *káçke kta*, he will bind, *kaçká*pi *kta*, they will bind. All other distinctions of number and tense are indicated in these two languages by adverbs, or by the general context of the sentence.

In lieu of these scant and imperfect modes of expression, the Tutelo gives us a surprising wealth of verbal forms. The distinction of singular and plural is clearly shown in all the persons, thus:

opēwa, he goes	*opehéhla*, they go
oyapēwa, thou goest	*oyapepūa*, ye go
owapēwa, I go	*maopēwa*, we go

Of tenses there are many forms. The termination in *ēwa* appears to be of an aorist, or rather of an indefinite sense. *Opēwa* (from *opa*, to go) may signify both he goes and he went. A distinctive present is indicated by the termination *ōma*; a distinctive past by *ōka*; and a future by *ta* or *ēta*. Thus from *ktē*, to kill, we have *waktēwa*, I kill him, or killed him, *wakteōma*; I am killing him, and *waktēta*, I will kill him. So *ohāta*, he sees it, becomes

57

ohatiōka, he saw it formerly, and *ohatēta*, he will see it. *Opēwa*, he goes (or went), becomes *opēta*, he will go, inflected as follows:

opēta, he will go
oyapēta, thou wilt go
owapēta, I will go

opehéhla, they will go
oyapétepa, ye will go
maopēta, we will go

The inflections for person and number in the distinctively present tense, ending in *oma*, are shown in the following example :

waginōma, he is sick
wayiñginoma, thou art sick
wameginōma, I am sick

waginónhna, they are sick
wayiñginómpo, ye are sick
mañgwaginōma, we are sick

Ohāta, he sees it, is thus varied :

ohata, he sees it
oyahata, thou seest it
owahata, I see it

ohatéhla, they see it
oyahatbua, ye see it
maohata, we see it

ohatiōka, he saw it
oyahatiōka, thou sawest it
owahatiōka, I saw it

ohatiokehla, they saw it
oyahatiokewa, ye saw it
maohatioka, we saw it

ohatēta, he will see it
oyahatēta, thou wilt see it
owahatēta, I shall see it

ohatetéhla, they will see it
oyahātetbūa, ye will see it
maohātēta, we shall see it

The following examples will show the variations of person in the aorist tense:

hahēwa, he says
hayihēwa, thou sayest
hawahēwa, I say

hahéhla, they say
hayihēpua, ye say
hamañkhēwa, we say

58

kīhnindēwa, he is hungry	*kīhnindēse,* they are hungry
yikīhnindēwa, thou art hungry	*kīhnindēpūa*, ye are hungry
mikīhnindēwa, I am hungry	*mahkihnindēwa*, we are hungry.

Wakoñspēwa, I remember it, an aorist form, becomes in the preterite *wakoñspeōka*, and, in the future, *wakoñspēta*. It is thus varied in the aorist and past tenses:

wakoñspēwa, I remember it	*makikoñspēwa*, we remember it
yakoñspēwa, thou rememberest it	*yakoñspepūa*, ye remember it
kikonspewa, he remembers it	*kikoñspēhĕla*, they remember it
wakoñspeōka, I remembered it	*makikoñspeōka*, we remembered it
yakoñspeōka, thou rememberedst it	*yakoñspepuyoka*, ye remembered it
kikoñspēoka, he remembered it	*kikoñspeleōka*, they remembered it

In several instances verbs were heard only in the inflected forms. For the simple or root-form, which doubtless exists in the language, we are obliged to have recourse to the better known Dakota language. Thus *opewa*, he went, and *opeta*, he will go, indicate a root *opa*, he goes, which is actually found in the Dakota.

So *manōma* (which is probably a distinctively present tense), and *manondañi*, both meaning he steals, indicate a briefer root-form which we find in the Dakota *manoñ*, having the same meaning. *Manōma*, which is probably a contraction of *manoñōma*, is thus varied:

manōma, he steals	*manoñnese*, they steal
yimanōma, thou stealest	*yimanompūa*, ye steal
mamanōma, I steal	*mañkmanōma*, we steal

From these examples it is evident that there are variations of inflection, which, if the language were better

59

understood, might probably be classified in distinct conjugations. Other instances of these variations will be given hereafter.

It is well known that in the Iroquois, Algonquin, Cherokee, and other Indian languages, of different stocks, there are many forms of the verb, negative, interrogative, desiderative, and the like, which are among the most notable characteristics of these languages, and add much to their power of expression. The Tutelo has several of these forms, but none of them are found in the Dakota or Hidatsa, both of which express the meaning of these forms by adverbial phrases or other circumlocutions. The negative form in Tutelo is made (in a manner which reminds us of the French *ne-pas*) by prefixing *k* or *ki* to the affirmative and suffixing *na*. The tense terminations *oma*, *owa*, and *ewa*, become *ona* and *ena* in this form :

inksēha, he laughs	*kinkséhna*, he does not laugh
iñwaksēha, I laugh	*kiñwahsehna*, I do not laugh
wameginōma, I am sick	*kiwameginōna*, I am not sick
waktēwa, I killed him	*kiwaktēna*, I did not kill him
owaklāka, I speak	*kowaklākna*, I do not speak
wakteōma, I am killing him	*kiwakteōna*, I am not killing him
yahōwa, he is coming	*kiahōna*, he is not coming

Kiñkséhna, he is not laughing, is thus varied in the present tense :

kiñkséhna, he is not laughing	*kiñksehanēna*, they are not laughing
kiñyakséhna, thou art not laughing	*kiñyakséhpuna*, ye are not laughing
kiñwakséhna, I am not laughing	*kimaeñkséhna*, we are not laughing

The interrogative form terminates in *o*, as :

yaktēwa, thou killedst him	*yaktēwo*, didst thou kill him?
yakteoma, thou art killing him	*yakteoñmo*, art thou killing him?
yatēta, thou wilt kill him	*yaktēto*, wilt thou kill him ?
yatīwa, thou dwellest	*toka yatiwo*, where dost thou dwell?
alēwa, he is going	*toka alewo*, where is he going?

It is evident that this form is an inflection, pure and simple. It is a vowel change, and not in any manner an agglutinated particle. It takes the place of that elevation of tone with which we conclude an interrogative sentence, and which, strange to say, is not heard among the Dakotas. Mr. Riggs remarks that "unlike the English, the voice falls at the close of all interrogative sentences."

The desiderative form appears to be expressed by the affixed particle *bi* or *be*, but the examples which were obtained happened to be all in the negative, thus :

owapēwa, I go	*kowapēbina*, I do not wish to go
opetēse, he is going, or will go	*kopēbenīse*, he does not wish to go
hawilewa, I come	*kiwilēbina*, I do not wish to come
waktewa, I kill him	*kiwaktēbina*, I do not wish to kill him

The imperative mood is distinguished apparently by a sharp accent on the final syllable of the verb, which loses the sign of tense. Thus from the *ñgō*, to give (in Dakota and Hidatsa, *ku*), which appears in *maingōwa*, I give to you, we have, in the imperative, *masā mingó*, give me a knife. *kitēse* or *kitesel*, he kills him, gives *kité tçoñki*, or *tçoñk' kité*, kill the dog.

61

In the western languages of the Dakota stock, certain particles prefixed to the verb play an important part in modifying the meaning. Thus in Dakota and Hidatsa the prefix *pa* signifies that the action is done with the hand. From *ksa*, Dak., meaning separate, we have *paksá*, to break with the hand; from *qu*, Hid., to spill, *paqu*, to pour out with the hand. The Dakota *na*, Hidatsa *ada* (for *ana*) are prefixes showing that the action is done with the foot. The Dakota *ya*, Hidatsa *da* (often pronounced *ra* or *la*) show that the act is done with the mouth. *Ka* (Dak.) and *dăk* (Hid.) indicate an act done by a sudden, forcible impulse, &c. Attempts were made to ascertain whether similar prefixes were employed in the Tutelo speech. It was found that in many cases the latter had distinct words to express acts which in the western languages were indicated by these compound forms. Still, a sufficient number of examples were obtained to show that the use of modifying prefixes was not unknown to the language. Thus the root *kusa*, which, evidently corresponds with the Dakota *ksa*, signifying separation, occurs in the following forms :

nantkūsisel, he breaks it off with the foot
latkūsisel, he bites it off
tikūsisel, he breaks it off by pushing
lakatkūsisel, he cuts it off with an axe

The Dakota *na*, signifying action with the foot, is evidently found, with some modification, in the Tutelo *nantkūsisel* above quoted, and also in *nañkōkisek*, to stamp with the foot, and in *konaqlōtisel*, to scratch with the foot. So the cutting, pushing, or impulsive prefix, *lak* or *laka*, which appears in *lakatkūsisel*, is found also in *lakatkūsisel*, he cuts open, *lakaspēta*, to cut off in pieces, *lakasāse*, to chop, *lakapleh*, to sweep the floor. *La*, which in *latkūsisel* indicates action with the mouth, is found also in *lakpēse*, to drink, and perhaps in *yilanāha*, to count or read, which has the corresponding prefix *ya* in the Dakota word *yāwa*, of like meaning.

The affixed or incorporated pronouns are used with transitive verbs to form what are called by the Spanish writers on Indian grammar *transitions*, that is, to express the passage of the action from the agent or subject to the object. This usage is governed by very simple rules. In the Dakota and Hidatsa the rule prevails, that when two affixed pronouns come together, the one being in the nominative case and the other in the objective, the objective always precedes the nominative, as in *mayakoçka* (Dak.) me-thou-bindest, *dimakiděci* (Hid.) thee-I-love. In the Dakota the third personal pronoun is in general not expressed; *kaçká* signifies both he binds, and he binds him, her, or it; *wakáçka* is I bind, and I bind him, &c. In the Hidatsa, this pronoun is not expressed in the nominative, but in the objective it is indicated by the pronoun *i* prefixed to the verb, as *kiděçi*, he loves ; *ikideçi*, he loves him, her or it.

The Tutelo, as far as could be ascertained, follows the usage of the Dakota in regard to the third personal pronoun (which is not expressed) but differs from both the other languages, at least in some instances, in the order of the pronouns. The nominative affix occasionally precedes the objective, as in MAYI*newa*, I-thee-see. Yet in *kohi-*

*nañk*WIYA*hewa*, me-thou-struckest (where the pronouns are inserted), this order is reversed. The rule on which these variations depend was not ascertained. Owing to the difficulties of an inquiry carried on through the medium of a double translation (from English into Cayuga or Onondaga, and from the latter into Tutelo), it was not easy to gain a clear idea of the precise meaning of many of the examples which were obtained. An Indian when asked to translate "I love thee," or "thou lovest me," unless he is an educated man, or perfectly familiar with the language in which he is addressed, is apt to become perplexed, and to reverse the meaning of the pronouns. The following examples, however, will suffice to show that the system of transitions exists in the Tutelo, though they do not enable us to analyze and reconstruct it completely. Many other examples were obtained, but are omitted from a doubt of their correctness.

> *wakteōma*, I am killing him
> *waikteōma* (for *wayikteōma*) I am killing thee
> *mikteōma*, he is killing me
> *yakteōma*, thou art killing him
> *kiteóñsel*, he is killing them
>
> *inēwa*, he sees him (or he saw him)
> *minēwa*, I see him (qu. *m'inēwa*, for *ma-inēwa*)
> *mayinēwa*, I see thee
> *miinēwa*, he sees me
> *yiinēwa*, he sees thee
> *miinéhla*, they see me
>
> *yandostēka*, he loves him
> *yandomistēka*, he loves me
> *yandoyistēka*, he loves thee

yandowastēka, I love him
yandoyastēka, thou lovest him
yandoyistēka, he loves thee
mankĭandostēka (qu. *maikiandoyistēka*), we love thee
maihiandostekanēse, we love them
waiyandostēka, he loves us
waiyandoyastēka, thou loved us
yandostekanēse, he loves them (or they love him)
yandomistēkana, they love me

kohinañhīwa, he struck (or strikes) him
kohinañkyihīwa, he struck thee
kohinañmihīwa, he struck me

kohinañwahīwa, I struck him
kohinañyahīwa, thou struckest him
kohinañkwiyahīwa, thou struckest me
kohinañmañkihīwa, we struck him

gikōha (or *kikōha*), he calls to him
wigikōha, I call to him
waingikōha, (for *wayingikōha*), I call to thee
iñgikohīse (for *yingikohīse*), he calls to thee
iñgikopolēse, he calls to you
miñgikoha, he calls to me
yigikoha, thou callest to him
ingikopūa, they call to you
gikohanēse, they call to them

From the foregoing examples it is evident that the system of transitions in the Tutelo is as complete as in the Dakota and Hidatsa. But there are apparently some peculiar euphonic changes, and some of the pronouns are indicated by terminal inflections, particularly in the second person plural and in the third person singular and plural.

In the Tutelo, as in the Dakota and Hidatsa, substantives and adjectives are readily converted into neuter verbs by the addition or insertion of the pronouns and the verbal suffixes. It is in this manner that these languages, like other Indian tongues, are generally enabled to dispense with the use of the substantive verb. Thus in the Dakota *witçaçta*, man, by inserting the pronoun *ma*, I, becomes *wimatçaçta* or *witçamaçta*, I am a man, and by inserting *uñ* (we) and adding the plural affix *pi*, becomes *wiuñtçaçtapi*, we are men. So also *waçte*, good, becomes *mawaçte*, I am good, *uñwaçtepi*, we are good.

In the Tutelo the word *wahtāka*, or *wahtākai*, man, is inflected as follows:

> *wamihtākai*, I am a man.
> *wayihtākai*, thou art a man.
> *wahtākai*, he is a man.
> *miwamihtākai*, we are men.
> *iñwahtākai*, ye are men.
> *hūkwahtākai*, they are men.

The last two forms appear not to be regular, and may have been given by mistake. *Hūkwahtākai* probably means "all are men."

This verb may take the aorist form, as :

> *wamihtakāwa*, I am (or was) a man.
> *wayihtakāwa*, thou art (or wast) a man.
> *wahtakāwa*, he is (or was) a man, &c.

So the adjective *bī*, good, becomes, with the aorist affix *wa*, *bīwa*, he is (or was) good; *yimbīwa*, thou art good; *mimbīwa*, I am. good. In the present tense we have *ebīse*, he is good ; *ebilēse*, they are good ; and in the preterit, *ebikōa*, he was good.

Adverbs.

In many cases, as has been already shown, the English adverb is indicated in the Tutelo by a modification of the verb. The negative adverb, for example, is usually expressed in this manner, as in *iñkseha* he is laughing, *kiñksehna*, he is not laughing ; *migītowe*, it is mine, *kimigītonañ*, it is not mine.

Sometimes the meaning which in English would be expressed by an adverb accompanying a verb, is expressed in Tutelo by two verbs. Thus we have *ihōha*, she is sewing, apparently from a root *ihō* or *yehō*, to sew; and *koñspēwa yehō*, she is sewing well, *i.e.*, she is careful in sewing (lit., she thinks, or remembers, in sewing); *kebīna yehō*, she is sewing badly, *i.e.* she does not well in sewing (or is not good at sewing). Here *kebīna* is the negative form of *biwa*, he (or she) is good.

Prepositions.

Many phrases were obtained with a view of ascertaining the prepositions of the Tutelo, but without success. Sometimes an expression which in English requires a preposition would in the Tutelo appear as a distinct word. Thus, while *ati* signifies a house, *tokai* was given as equivalent to "in the house." It may perhaps simply mean "at home." Prairie is *latāhkoi*, but *onīi* signifies "at the prairie."

Other examples would seem to show that the prepositions in the Tutelo, as in the Hidatsa, and to a large extent in the Dakota, are incorporated with the verb. Thus *tāhkai* signifies "woods," and *tāhkai aginēse*, he is in the woods. So *sūi*, hill, and *sūi aginēse*, he is on the hill. The phrase "I am going to the house" was rendered *wilēta iatī*, and the phrase "I am coming from the house," by *waklēta iatī*. The practice of combining the preposition with the verb is very common in the Indian languages, which merely carry to a greater extent a familiar usage of the Aryan speech. The expressions, to ascend or descend a hill, to circumnavigate a lake, to overhang a fence, to undermine a wall, are examples of an idiom so prevalent in the Indian tongues as to supersede not merely the cases of nouns, but to a large extent the separable prepositions.

Conjunctions.

In the Tutelo, conjunctions appear to be less frequently used than in English. An elliptical form of speech is employed, but with no loss of clearness. The phrase "when I came, he was asleep," is expressed briefly *wihīok, hiañka*, I came, he was asleep. So, "I called the dog, but he did not come," becomes *wagelākiok tçoñk, kihūna*, I called the dog, he came not. When it is considered necessary or proper, however, the conjunction is expressed, as *kuminēna, mi Jān hinēka*, I did not see him, but John saw him. Here "but" is expressed by *mi*.

Nigás signifies "and," or "also." *Waklumīha lubūs nigás maséñ*, I bought a hat and a knife. *Owakiōka waktāka nigás mihéñ nomba lek*, I met a man and two women.

68

Li, which expresses "if," appears to be combined with the verb, at least in pronunciation; thus: *Lihīok, wagelāgita,* If he comes, I will tell him ; *wihūta, Jan lihiōk,* I will come if John comes. It is noticeable in the last two examples that the accent or stress of voice in the word *lihiok,* if he comes, appears to vary with the position of the word in the sentence.

Syntax.

The only points of interest which were ascertained in regard to the syntax of the language related to the position of words in a sentence.

The adjective follows the noun which it qualifies, as *wahtake bī,* good man, *atī asāñ,* white house. The rule applies to the numerals, as *miháñ noñsa,* one woman, *atī noñbai,* two houses. In this respect the Tutelo conforms to the rule which prevails in the Dakota and Hidatsa languages, as well as in the dialects of the Iroquois stock. In the Algonkin languages, on the other hand, the adjective precedes the noun.

The position of the verb appears to be a matter of indifference. It sometimes precedes the noun expressing either the subject or the object, and sometimes follows it, the meaning being determined apparently, as in Latin, by the inflection. Thus "I see a man," is *minēwa waiwāq* (I see him a man) ; and "the man sees me" is *miinēwa waiwāq* (he sees me the man). *Tçoñko miñgō,* give me a dog; *kité tçoñki,* kill the dog. In the last example the change from *tçoñko* to *tçoñki* is apparently not a grammatical inflection, but is merely euphonic. The verb in the imperative mood sufficiently shows the speaker's meaning, and the position of the noun is a matter of emphasis. "A *dog* give me," not a knife; "*kill* the dog," don't let him escape.

A verb is placed after another verb to which it bears the relation expressed by our infinitive ; as *miñgiloqkō waktēta*, let me kill him (allow me, I will kill him). *Wakonta opēta*, I will make him go (I cause him he will go).

The euphonic changes which words undergo in construction with other words are as marked in this language as they are in the proper Dakota tongue, and seem to be often of a similar, if not identical, character in the two languages. Thus in Dakota the word *çuñka*, dog, becomes *çuñke* when a possessive pronoun is prefixed. In the Tutelo a similar change takes place when the position of the noun is altered; thus we have *tçoñko miñgō* give me a dog; *kitē tçoñki*, kill the dog. The terminal vowel is frequently dropped, and the consonant preceding it undergoes a change; thus in Dakota *yuza*, to hold, becomes *yus* in the phrase *yus majin*, to stand holding. In Tutelo *nahāmbi* (properly *nahāñbi*) or *nahābi*, day, becomes *nahāmp* (or *nahāp*), in *nahāmp lāli* (or *nahāp lali*), three days. In such instances the two words which are thus in construction are pronounced as though they formed a single word.

VOCABULARY.

Particular care was taken to obtain, as correctly as possible, all the words comprised in the comparative vocabulary adopted by Gallatin for his Synopsis of the Indian languages. Many other words, expressive of the most common objects or actions, have been added. The alphabetical arrangement is adopted for convenience of reference, in lieu of the different order which Gallatin preferred for the purposes of his work. The Dakota and Hidatsa words are derived from the dictionaries of Mr. Riggs and Dr. Matthews, with the necessary changes of orthography which are required for the direct comparison of the three languages.

When several words are given in the Tutelo list, they are sometimes, as will be seen, mere variations of pronunciation or of grammatical form, and sometimes entirely distinct expressions. The Tutelo has no less than four words for "man," *wahtāka*, *waiyūwa* (or *waiwaq*), *yūhkañ*, and *nōna*, which have doubtless different shades of meaning, though these were not ascertained. There are also two distinct words meaning "to see," *inēwa*, and *ohāta*, and two for "go," *opēwa* and *qala* (or, rather *opa* and *la*, answering to *opa* and *ya* in Dakota). A more complete knowledge of the language would doubtless afford the means of discriminating between these apparently synonymous terms.

The words marked N in the vocabulary are those which were received from Nikonha himself. The pronunciation of these words may be accepted as that of a Tutelo of the full blood, and as affording a test of the correctness of the others.

—Horatio Hale, 1886.

TUTELO—ENGLISH

Agegaspe, *sixteen.*

Agegīsai, *fifteen.*

Agekisañka, *nineteen.*

Agelali, *thirteen.*

Agenomba, *twelve.*

Agenosai, *eleven.*

Agepalāli, *eighteen.*

Agesagōmi, *seventeen.*

Agetoba, *fourteen.*

Āgōdē, *shoes.*

Āgōre, *shoes.*

Agùs, *six* (N).

Ahá, *yes.*

Aháñ, *yes.*

Āk, *hand.*

Akásp, *six.*

Akāspei, *six.*

Akāteka, *warm.*

Akātia, *warm.*

Akekisāi, *fifteen.*

Akinosai, *eleven.*

Akipalāni, *eighteen.*

Akitopa, *fourteen.*

Alapōk, *ashes.*

Amāi, *earth.*

Amāni, *earth.*

Añgohlēi, *shoes.*

Añktāka, *weave.*

Aōma, *make*.
Aōñ, *make*.
Asai, *white*.
Asañi, *white*.
Asei, *white*.
Asépi, *black*.
Āskai, *near*.
Asōti, *blue*.
Asùñi, *white* (N).
Asùp, *black* (N).
Atçūt, *red*.
Atçūti, *red*.
Atī, *house* (N).
Atkasusai, *toes*.
Atsūti, *red*.
Awāqa, *yes*.

Bi, *good*.
Bīwa, *good*.
Butçk, *ten*.

Çūqe, *mountain*.

E, *him*.
Eāti, *father*.
Ebī, *good* (N).
Ei, *him*.
Eīñgă, *God*.

Ēiñgyeñ, *God.*
Ekuñi, *grandfather.*
Enī, *alive.*
Ērutāoñe, *warrior.*
Esái, *himself.*
Ētuk, *which.*

Gelāki, *call (v. A.).*
Gitonnēsel, *their.*
Gutskai, *boy.*

Hāg, *hand* (N).
Hahēwa, *say (v), speak.*
Hāk, *finger.*
Hāki, *hand.*
Handisonōi, *shoes* (N).
Hantá, *run (v)* (N).
Hasisiāi, *raspberry.*
Haspahínuk, *strawberry.*
Hāwōhā, *rain.*
Heistañ, *duck.*
Henā, *mother.*
Henùñ, *mother.*
Hetōa, *who.*
Hi, *thee.*
Hī, *come.*
Hianta, *sleep (v).*
Hiantkapewa, *sleep (v).*

Hiçto, *arm* (N).

Hīehā, *to boil.*

Higūñ, *grandfather, grandmother.*

Hinda, *run (v).*

Hisép, *axe.*

Hisēpi, *axe.*

Histēk, *island.*

Histéki, *stone.*

Histo, *arm.*

Hīyăñ, *sleep (v)* (N).

Hōakāi, *old.*

Hōhka, *old.*

Hohnùñk, *cranberry.*

Hōk, *all.*

Howa, *come.*

Hūk, *all.*

I, *he, him.*

Iap, *buffalo.*

Içi, *foot* (N).

Īçtai, *duck* (N).

Ieksā, *leg.*

Iētañ, *sea.*

Īh, *mouth* (N).

Ihao, *no.*

Iheñstek, *pipe (qu "mouth-stone").*

Ihī, *mouth.*

Ihī, *tooth* (N).

Ihīrtik, *pipe.*

Ihōha, *sew (v).*

Im, *he.*

Imahese, *they.*

Īnā, *mother* (N).

Inausíngā, *burn (v. a.).*

Inēwa, *see (v).*

Iñginumbai, *brother.*

Inī, *alive.*

Inīna, *alive.*

Īñkçe, *laugh* (N).

Inksēha, *laugh.*

Iñktēi, *near.*

Inōsek, *bow (n)* (N).

Inōsīk, *bow (n).*

Ipī, *good, handsome.*

Ipīkam, *handsome.*

Isáñi, *himself.*

Isī, *foot.*

Istihiōi, *beard.*

Itāi, *strong.*

Itāñ, *great.*

Itáñi, *great* (N).

Kāhi, *crow* (N).

Kainstākai, *crane.*

Kakāñwā, *what is that?*

Kanahābnen, *morning.*

Kanahāmpuai, *morning.*

Kasā, *five* (N).

Kasāñkai, *nine.*

Ketçi, *dance (v).*

Ketoa, *who.*

Kihnindewa, *hunger (v).*

Kiklēse, *awake.*

Kikōha, *call (v. a.).*

Kilomīha, *buy.*

Kisāháñi, *five.*

Kisāhi, *five.*

Kisañ, *five.*

Kisē, *five.*

Kitē, *kill* (N).

Kitēse, *kill.*

Kohinùnhiwa, *strike.*

Kōmqāñ, *girl* (N).

Koñspēwa, *remember, think.*

Konta, *cause (v).*

Kotskai, *small.*

Kotubós, *hat* (N).

Kowai, *there.*

Ksākai, *nine.*

Ksānk, *nine.*

Ktē, *kill.*

Kutçkai, *small* (N).

Kūtskai, *small.*

La, *go*.

Lākpē, *drink (v)*.

Lakaplék, *sweep (v)*.

Lakasāse, *chop (v)*.

Lakatkōsa, *cut (v) with knife*.

Lakatkūsisel, *to break with foot*.

Lāni, *three*.

Lapēta, *drink (v)*.

Lāt, *three*.

Latahkoi, *prairie*.

Latkūsisel, *to bite off*.

Letci, *tongue*.

Li, *if*.

Lubūs, *hat*.

Lūti, *eat*.

Ma, *I*.

Mae, *us, we*.

Maesāi, *ourselves*.

Māesáñ, *we*.

Maesáñi, *ourselves*.

Mahanañka, *sit*.

Mahēi, *woman*.

Maktukai, *wolf*.

Māmbī, *town*.

Maminkrē, *wind*.

Māmpā isī, *devil (evil spirit)*.

Mampamasawohōka, *churn (v)*.

Mampañdahkai, *buffalo*.

Māmpī, *town*.

Mamùnklēi, *wind*.

Mañ, *we*.

Māndāhkāi, *turkey*.

Mandaqēi, *maize*.

Māndùhkāi, *turkey*.

Manēasān, *goose*.

Manēasēi, *duck*.

Manī, *water* (N).

Maniñkiē, *wind* (N).

Māñki, *husband*.

Māñkōi, *arrow* (N).

Mañksīi, *arrow*.

Mañksūi, *bag*.

Manōma, *steal*.

Manoñ, *steal*.

Manotihūa, *fog*.

Mañs, *iron*.

Mañtōi, *sky*.

Maqgītowe, *ours*.

Maqōsi, *cloud* (N).

Mās, *iron*.

Masā, *knife*.

Masāi, *knife* (N).

Masēi, *knife*.

Maséñi, *knife*.

Masīqorāk, *iron*.

Maste, *spring* (N).

Mātāqē, *maize* (N).

Matōi, *sky*.

Matoñi, *sky*.

Mayeñgiéqta, *bird's nest*.

Māyīñk, *bird*.

Mayiñk pōs, *egg*.

Mayūtkāi, *pigeon*.

Meñkolahāpi, *canoe*.

Mentalōken, *my face*.

Mentasūi, *my eye*.

Mi, *but*.

Mi, *I, me*.

Mi, *sun*.

Mīe, *sun* (N).

Miéñ, *wood*.

Mīéñ, *tree*.

Migītowe, *mine*.

Mihañ, *woman* (N).

Mihañi, *wife*.

Miháñi, *woman*.

Mīm, *I, we*.

Mimahēi, *moon*.

Mīn, *sun* (N).

Mīñgiratçah, *ice*.

Mīnktē, *gun* (N).

Minagi, *book*.

Minēk, *sister* (N).

Minēk', *my uncle.*

Minī, *my leg.*

Miñkolhāpi, *canoe.*

Minōn, *my younger brother.*

Mīnōsā', *moon* (N).

Mintasēi, *my neck.*

Miohañk, *my daughter.*

Misāi, *I alone or I myself.*

Misáñi, *I alone or I myself.*

Miyēi, *wood.*

Miyeñi, *wood.*

Moñdi, *bear.*

Mōnti, *bear.*

Mūnti, *bear* (N).

Muktāgi, *grass.*

Munaqka, *beaver.*

Mùñktagín, *wolf* (N).

Mùnktōkāi, *wolf.*

Nahambe, *day.*

Nahámblekéñ, *today.*

Nahamp, *day.*

Nahampk, *to-morrow.*

Nahañpe, *day.*

Nahūh, *ear.*

Nān, *three* (N).

Nāni, *three.*

Nañka, *stay (v).*

Nañkōkisek, *stamp (v) with foot.*

Nañtói, *hair.*

Naqōq, *ear* (N).

Natói, *hair.*

Natónwe, *hair* (N).

Nei, *here.*

Nēikiñ, *this, that.*

Néke, *this.*

Netçi, *tongue.*

Netsi, *tongue.*

Niça, *speak* (N).

Nigás, *and.*

Nisēp, *axe* (N).

Nistāqkai, *squirrel.*

Nistēk, *stone* (N).

Niwāgenúmpai, *brother* (N).

Nomba, *two.*

Nomp, *two* (N).

Nōna, *man.*

Noñç, *one* (N).

Noñhi, *ice.*

Noñs, *one.*

Noñsa, *one.*

Nōq, *hail.*

Nosāi, *one.*

Oaki, *meet.*

Oaklaka, *speak.*

Ohāta, *see (v)*.

Ohēki, *mountain*.

Ohōn, *marry*.

Ohōteha, *marry*.

Ohsīha, *darkness*.

Okāyek, *bad* (N).

Okahōk, *all*.

Okāyik, *bad*.

Okeni, *hundred*.

Okeni butskai, *thousand*.

Oknahō, *work (v)*.

Olohī, *tie (v)*.

Oluskēse, *claw*.

Omaklēwa, *wind*.

Onī, *tree*.

Oñqyāyùñ, *valley*.

Opatañsel, *shoot off (v)*.

Opemīha, *think*.

Opewa, *go*.

Osī, *night*.

Osihitewa, *evening*.

Otō, *green* (N).

Otōi, *grass*.

Otōi, *leaf*.

Otolakōi, *green*.

Otōq, *leaf* (N).

Oyándise, *beg*.

Pahē, *pound (v).*

Palāli, *eight.*

Pālán, *eight* (N).

Palāni, *eight.*

Pania minte, *forehead.*

Pāqtē, *none.*

Paqti, *none.*

Pasūi, *head.*

Pasūye, *head* (N).

Penihēi, *copper.*

Pētç, *fire.*

Pēti, *fire.*

Pī, *good.*

Pirē, *handsome* (N).

Pītç, *fire* (N).

Pōtsk, *ten* (N).

Pūs, *cat* (N) (i.e. puss).

Putçka nani, *thirty.*

Putsk, *ten.*

Putskai, *ten.*

Putskáñi, *ten.*

Putska nomba, *twenty.*

Qaka, *weep.*

Qala, *go.*

Qāpi, *berk.*

Qāqise, *cry (v).*

Qawō, *rain.*

Qawōi, *rain* (N).
Qawōqa, *rain*.
Qūtçkai, *son*.

Sā, *nine*.
Sāgóm, *seven* (N).
Sagomēi, *seven*.
Sagomíñk, *seven*.
Sahéñta, *speak*.
Sahīta, *speak*.
Sāñ, *nine*.
Sanī, *cold*.
Sāsi, *bed*.
Sīi, *yellow*.
Sitō, *yesterday*.
Soti, *strong*.
Stēk, *island*.
Stestēki, *island*.
Sūhi, *mountain*.
Sui, *long*.
Sùnktāki, *grass* (N).
Sùntése, *bury*.

Tabunītçkai, *star* (N).
Tahañk, *sister*.
Tāhkāi, *forest*.
Tahoñtanēki, *have*.
Tä'i, *autumn*.

Taksīta, *river*.

Taksītai, *river*.

Talūkna, *face*.

Tāñyi, *autumn*.

Tapi, *ball*.

Tāpī, *heart*.

Tapniñskai, *star*.

Tarūbna, *face*.

Tasēi, *neck*.

Tāskahōi, *oak*.

Taskahūi, *oak* (N).

Tasūi, *eye*.

Tasūye, *eye* (N).

Tāt, *father* (N).

Tça, *nine* (N).

Tçoñg, *dog* (N).

Tçoñgo, *dog*.

Tçoñk, *dog*.

Tçoñki, *dog*.

Tçutçāg, *finger-nails*.

Tē, *dead*.

Tē, *die* (N).

Tēka, *dead*.

Tēkai, *son*.

Tēolāha, *die*.

Tēsi, *body*.

Tewakītùnwa, *whose*.

Tikōi, *forehead*.

Toba, *four.*

Tohkai, *fox.*

Tokā, *where.*

Tokēnāq, *when.*

Tokēnuñ, *how many.*

Tomīn, *aunt.*

Tōp, *four* (N).

Tōpa, *four.*

Topai, *four.*

Tsāen, *nine* (N).

Tsutsāki, *finger-nails.*

Tūhangrūa, *thunder.*

Tūi, *thunder.*

Ukāyik, *bad.*

Ukāyik, *ugly.*

Ukenī mbutskai, *thousand.*

Ukenī, *hundred.*

Ùkstéh, *cheek.*

Usī, *night.*

Usīhaa, *darkness.*

Wae, *us.*

Wae, *we.*

Wāgatç, *girl* (N).

Wāgenī, *snake.*

Wagesākwāi, *bread.*

Waginōma, *sick.*

Wagitçi, *dance (v)* (N).
Wāglumihínta, *buy.*
Wāgotskāi, *child.*
Wahīik, *my elder brother.*
Wahōi, *bone.*
Wahtahka, *man.*
Wahtākai, *Indian (man).*
Wahūi, *bone.*
Waitiwa, *boy.*
Waiwaq, *man.*
Wāiyuā, *man* (N).
Waiyūwa, *man.*
Wakasīk, *boy* (N).
Wakasīk, *child, girl.*
Wāksākpāi, *bread.*
Walūti, *food.*
Wānēi, *winter.*
Wāneñi, *winter.*
Wanùntçī, *ghost.*
Waqēta, *see (v).*
Wasōti, *brain.*
Wāste, *pine-tree* (N).
Wāstī, *pine-tree.*
Wasūt, *brain.*
Watai, *beads.*
Watemai, *aunt.*
Wāyī, *blood* (N).
Wayōtkāi, *pigeon.*

Wāyupāki, *strong.*

Wāyuqtéki, *flesh.*

Wayūqtik, *flesh.*

Wehaéhimpē, *spring* (N).

Wehahempēi, *spring* (N).

Wēhē piwa, *summer.*

Wi, *me.*

Wiéñ, *tree* (N).

Wihoi, *fish* (N).

Wiohañke, *my daughter.*

Wisuñtk, *my younger brother.*

Witāhe, *friend.*

Witāi, *deer.*

Wital, *my elder brother.*

Witañsk, *my elder brother.*

Witaqā, *friend.*

Witēka, *my daughter* (N).

Witēka, *son* (N).

Wustetkai, *partridge.*

Ya, *thou.*

Yahan, *no.*

Yahūa, *come.*

Yalēwa, *walk (v).*

Yāmùñiyē, *sing (v)* (N).

Yandowasteka, *love.*

Yanti, *heart.*

Yāñti, *heart* (N).

Yāop, *beaver* (N).

Yapóske, *long* (N).

Yāt, *father* (N).

Ye, *thou.*

Yehēti, *club.*

Yēhī, *beard.*

Yehíñstik, *pipe* (N).

Yéhni, *tobacco.*

Yeksā, *leg* (N).

Yeksāi, *leg.*

Yéñki, *young.*

Yesáñi, *thyself.*

Yesiñk, *kettle.*

Yetāi, *sea.*

Yetañi, *sea.*

Yi, *thee.*

Yihnū, *tobacco.*

Yilanāha, *count (v).*

Yim, *ye.*

Yīm, *thou.*

Yiñgītambūi, *your (pl).*

Yiñgītowe, *thine.*

Yisái, *thyself.*

Yohiñk, *berk.*

Yosañkrota, *cherry.*

Yūqtéki, *body.*

Yuhkañ, *man.*

Yukān, *that.*

Yumpañkatska, *long.*

ENGLISH—TUTELO

Alive, *enī, inī, inīna*.

All, *hūk, hōk, okahōk*.

And, *nigás*.

Arm, *hiçto* (N), *histo*.

Arrow, *māñkōi* (N), *mañksīi*.

Ashes, *alapōk*.

Aunt, *tomīn, watemai*.

Autumn, *tä'i, tāñyi*.

Awake, *kiklēse*.

Axe, *hisép, hisēpi, nisēp* (N).

Bad, *okāyek* (N), *okāyik, ukāyik*.

Bag, *mañksūi*.

Ball, *tapi*.

Berk, *qāpi, yohiñk*.

Bear, *moñdi, mōnti, mūnti* (N).

Beads, *watai*.

Beard, *istihiōi, yēhī*.

Beaver, *munaqka, yāop* (N).

Bed, *sāsi*.

Beg, *oyándise*.

Bird, *māyīñk*.

Bird's nest, *mayeñgiéqta*.

Bite, to bite off, *latkūsisel*.

Black, *asépi, asùp* (N).

Blood, *wāyī* (N).

Blue, *asōti*.

Body, *tēsi, yūqtéki*.

Boil, to, *hīehā.*

Bone, *wahōi, wahūi.*

Book, *minagi.*

Boy, *gutskai, waitiwa, wakasīk* (N).

Bow (n), *inōsek* (N), *inōsīk.*

Brain, *wasōti, wasūt.*

Bread, *wagesākwāi, wāksākpāi.*

Break, to break with foot, *lakatkūsisel.*

Brother, *iñginumbai, niwāgenúmpai* (N).   **My elder brother**, *wahīik, wital, witañsk.* **My younger brother**, *minōn, wisuñtk.*

Buffalo, *iap, mampañdahkai.*

Burn (v. a.), *inausíngā.*

Bury, *sùntése.*

But, *mi.*

Buy, *kilomīha, wāglumihínta.*

Call (v. a.), *gelāki, kikōha.*

Canoe, *meñkolahāpi, miñkolhāpi.*

Cat, *pūs* (N).

Cause (v), *konta.*

Cheek, *ùkstéh.*

Cherry, *yosañkrota.*

Child, *wāgotskāi, wakasīk.*

Chop (v), *lakasāse.*

Churn (v), *mampamasawohōka.*

Claw, *oluskēse.*

Cloud, *maqōsi* (N).

Club, *yehēti*.
Cold, *sanī*.
Come, *hī*, *howa*, *yahūa*.
Copper, *penihēi*.
Count (v), *yilanāha*.
Cranberry, *hohnùñk*.
Crane, *kainstākai*.
Crow (n), *kāhi*.
Cry (v), *qāqise*.
Cut (v) with knife, *lakatkōsa*.

Dance (v), *ketçi*, *wagitçi* (N).
Darkness, *ohsīha*, *usīhaa*.
My daughter, *miohañk*, *wiohañke*, *witēka* (N).
Day, *nahambe*, *nahamp*, *nahañpe*.
Dead, *tē*, *tēka*.
Deer, *witāi*.
Devil (evil spirit), *māmpā isī*.
Die, *tē* (N), *tēolāha*.
Dog, *tçoñg* (N), *tçoñgo*, *tçoñk*, *tçoñki*.
Drink (v), *lākpē*, *lapēta*.
Duck, *heistañ*, *īçtai* (N), *manēasēi*.

Ear, *nahūh*, *naqōq* (N).
Earth, *amāi*, *amāni*.
Eat, *lūti*.
Egg, *mayiñk pōs*.
Eight, *palāli*, *pālán* (N), *palāni*.
Eighteen, *agepalāli*, *akipalāni*.

Eleven, *agenosai, akinosai.*
Evening, *osihitewa.*
Eye, *tasūi, tasūye* (N). **My eye**, *mentasūi.*

Face, *talūkna, tarūbna.* **My face**, *mentalōken.*
Father, *eāti, tāt* (N), *yāt* (N),
Fifteen, *agegīsai, akekisāi.*
Finger, *hāk.*
Finger-nails, *tsutsāki, tçutçāg.*
Fire, *pētç, pēti, pītç* (N).
Fish, *wihoi* (N).
Five, *kasā* (N), *kisāhi, kisāháñi, kisañ, kisē.*
Flesh, *wāyuqtéki, wayūqtik.*
Fog, *manotihūa.*
Food, *walūti.*
Foot, *içi* (N), *isī.*
Forehead, *pania minte, tikōi.*
Forest, *tāhkāi.*
Four, *toba, tōp* (N), *tōpa, topai.*
Fourteen, *agetoba, akitopa.*
Fox, *tohkai.*
Friend, *witāhe, witaqā.*

Ghost, *wanùntçī.*
Girl, *kōmqāñ* (N), *wāgatç* (N), *wakasīk.*
Go, *la, opewa, qala.*
God, *eīñgǎ, ēiñgyeñ.*
Good, *bi, bīwa, ebī* (N), *ipī, pī.*

100

Goose, *manēasān.*
Grandfather, *ekuñi, higūñ.*
Grandmother, *higūñ.*
Grass, *muktāgi, otōi, sùnktāki* (N).
Great, *itāñ, itáñi* (N).
Green, *otō* (N), *otolakōi.*
Gun, *mīnktē* (N).

Hail, *nōq.*
Hair, *nañtói, natói, natónwe* (N).
Hand, *āk, hāg* (N), *hāki.*
Handsome, *ipī, ipīkam, pirē* (N).
Have, *tahoñtanēki.*
Hat, *kotubós* (N), *lubūs.*
He, *i, im.*
Head, *pasūi, pasūye* (N).
Heart, *tāpī, yanti, yāñti* (N).
Here, *nei.*
Him, *e, ei, i.*
Himself, *esái, isáñi.*
House, *atī* (N).
How many, *tokēnuñ.*
Hundred, *okeni, ukenī.*
Hunger (**v**), *kihnindewa.*
Husband, *māñki.*

I, *ma, mi, mīm.* **I alone or I myself**, *misāi, misáñi.*
Ice, *mīñgiratçah, noñhi.*

If, *li*.
Indian (man), *wahtākai*.
Iron, *mañs*, *mās*, *masīqorāk*.
Island, *histēk*, *stēk*, *stestēki*.

Kettle, *yesiñk*.
Kill, *kitē* (N), *kitēse*, *ktē*.
Knife, *masā*, *masāi* (N), *masēi*, *maséñi*.

Laugh, *īñkçe* (N), *inksēha*.
Leaf, *otōi*, *otōq* (N).
Leg, *ieksā*, *yeksā* (N), *yeksāi*. **My leg**, *minī*.
Long, *sui*, *yapóske* (N), *yumpañkatska*.
Love, *yandowasteka*.

Maize, *mandaqēi*, *mātāqē* (N).
Make, *aōma*, *aōñ*.
Man, *nōna*, *wahtahka*, *waiwaq*, *wāiyuā* (N), *waiyūwa*,
  yuhkañ.
Marry, *ohōn*, *ohōteha*.
Me, *mi*, *wi*.
Meet, *oaki*.
Mine, *migītowe*.
Moon, *mimahēi*, *mīnōsā'* (N).
Morning, *kanahābnen*, *kanahāmpuai*.
Mother, *henā*, *henùñ*, *īnā* (N).
Mountain, *çūqe*, *ohēki*, *sūhi*.
Mouth, *īh* (N), *ihī*.

Near, *āskai, iñktēi.*
Neck, *tasēi.* **My neck**, *mintasēi.*
Night, *osī, usī.*
Nine, *kasāñkai, ksākai, ksānk, sā, sāñ, tça* (N), *tsāen* (N).
Nineteen, *agekisañka.*
No, *ihao, yahan.*
None, *pāqtē, paqti.*

Oak, *tāskahōi, taskahūi* (N).
Old, *hōakāi, hōhka.*
One, *noñç* (N), *noñs, noñsa, nosāi.*
Ours, *maqgītowe.*
Ourselves, *maesāi, maesáñi.*

Partridge, *wustetkai.*
Pigeon, *mayūtkāi, wayōtkāi.*
Pine-tree, *wāste* (N), *wāstī.*
Pipe *iheñstek, ihīrtik, yehíñstik* (N). (qu, "mouth-stone")
Pound (v), *pahē.*
Prairie, *latahkoi.*

Rain, *hāwōhā, qawō, qawōi* (N), *qawōqa.*
Raspberry, *hasisiāi.*
Red, *atçūt, atçūti, atsūti.*
Remember, *koñspēwa.*
River, *taksīta, taksītai.*
Run (v), *hantá* (N), *hinda.*

Say (v), *hahēwa*.

Sea, *iētañ*, *yetāi*, *yetañi*.

See (v), *inēwa*, *ohāta*, *waqēta*.

Seven, *sāgóm* (N), *sagomēi*, *sagomíñk*.

Seventeen, *agesagōmi*.

Sew (v), *ihōha*.

Shoes, *āgōdē*, *āgōre*, *añgohlēi*, *handisonōi* (N).

Shoot off (v), *opatañsel*.

Sick, *waginōma*.

Sing (v), *yāmùñiyē* (N).

Sister, *minēk* (N), *tahañk*.

Sit, *mahanañka*.

Six, *agùs* (N), *akásp*, *akāspei*.

Sixteen, *agegaspe*.

Sky, *mañtōi*, *matōi*, *matoñi*.

Sleep (v), *hianta*, *hiantkapewa*, *hīyǎñ* (N)

Small, *kotskai*, *kutçkai*, *kūtskai*.

Snake, *wāgenī*.

Son, *tēkai*, *qūtçkai*, *witēka* (N).

Speak, *hahēwa*, *niça* (N), *oaklaka*, *sahéñta*, *sahīta*.

Spring (n), *maste*, *wehaéhimpē*, *wehahempēi*.

Squirrel, *nistāqkai*.

Stamp (v) **with foot**, *nañkōkisek*.

Star, *tabunītçkai* (N), *tapniñskai*.

Stay (v), *nañka*.

Steal, *manōma*, *manoñ*.

Stone, *histéki*, *nistēk* (N).

Strawberry, *haspahínuk*.

Strike, *kohinùnhiwa*.

Strong, *itāi*, *soti*, *wāyupāki*.

Summer, *wēhē piwa*.

Sun, *mi*, *mīe* (N), *mīn* (N).

Sweep (v), *lakaplék*.

Ten, *butçk*, *pōtsk* (N), *putsk*, *putskai*, *putskáñi*.

That, *nēikiñ*, *yukān*.

Thee, *hi*, *yi*.

Their, *gitonnēsel*.

There, *kowai*.

They, *imahese*.

Thine, *yiñgītowe*.

Thirteen, *agelali*.

Thirty, *putçka nani*.

This, *nēikiñ*, *néke*.

Think, *koñspēwa*, *opemīha*.

Thou, *ya*, *ye*, *yīm*.

Thousand, *okeni butskai*, *ukenī mbutskai*.

Three, *lāt*, *lāni*, *nān* (N), *nāni*.

Thunder, *tūhangrūa*, *tūi*.

Thyself, *yesáñi*, *yisái*.

Tie (v), *olohī*.

Tobacco, *yéhni*, *yihnū*.

Today, *nahámblekéñ*.

Toes, *atkasusai*.

Tomorrow, *nahampk*.

Tongue, *letci*, *netçi*, *netsi*.

Tooth, *ihī* (N).

Town, *māmbī*, *māmpī*.

Tree, *mīéñ*, *onī*, *wiéñ* (N).

Turkey, *māndāhkāi*, *māndùhkāi*.

Twelve, *agenomba*.

Twenty, *putska nomba*.

Two, *nomba*, *nomp* (N).

Ugly, *ukāyik*.

Uncle, my, *minēk'*.

Us, *mae*, *wae*.

Valley, *oñqyāyùñ*.

Walk (v), *yalēwa*.

Warm, *akāteka*, *akātia*.

Warrior, *ērutāoñe*.

Water, *manī* (N).

We, *mae*, *māesáñ*, *mañ*, *mīm*, *wae*.

Weave, *añktāka*.

Weep, *qaka*.

Which, *ētuk*.

What is that?, *kakāñwā*.

When, *tokēnāq*.

Where, *tokā*.

White, *asai*, *asañi*, *asei*, *asùñi* (N).

Who, *hetōa*, *ketoa*.

Whose, *tewakītùnwa*.

Wife, *mihañi*.

Wind, *maminkrē, mamùnklēi, maniñkiē* (N), *omaklēwa*.

Winter, *wānēi, wāneñi*.

Wolf, *mùñktagín* (N), *mùnktōkāi, maktukai*.

Woman, *mahēi, mihañ* (N), *miháñi*.

Wood, *miéñ, miyēi, miyeñi*.

Work (v), *oknahō*.

Ye, *yim*.

Yellow, *sīi*.

Yes, *ahá, aháñ, awāqa*.

Yesterday, *sitō*.

Young, *yéñki*.

Your (pl), *yiñgītambūi*.

CLASSIFICATION OF THE SIOUAN LANGUAGES

EASTERN SIOUAN
   Catawba
   Woccon
WESTERN SIOUAN
   Missouri River
      Hidatsa
      Crow
   Mandan
   Mississippi Valley
      Dakotan
         Sioux
         Assiniboine
         Stoney
      Dhegiha
         Omaha-Ponca
         Osage
         Kansa
         Quapaw
      Chiwere-Winnebago
         Chiwere (Otoe, Missouri, Iowa)
         Winnebago
   Southeastern
      Ofo
      Biloxi
      Tutelo-Saponi

Sources: Carter 1980; Foster 1996; Goddard 1996.

Also available in the American Language Reprint Series

Volume 1. A Vocabulary of the Nanticoke Dialect
Volume 2. A Vocabulary of Susquehannock
Volume 3. A Vocabulary of the Unami Jargon
Volume 4. A Vocabulary of Powhatan
Volume 5. An Ancient New Jersey Indian Jargon
Volume 6. A Vocabulary of Tuscarora
Volume 7. A Vocabulary of Woccon
Volume 8. A Dictionary of Powhatan
Volume 9. A Vocabulary of Mohegan-Pequot
Volume 10. A Vocabulary of New Jersey Delaware
Volume 11. A Vocabulary of Stadaconan
Volume 12. Denny's Vocabulary of Delaware
Volume 13. A Vocabulary of Roanoke
Volume 14. Denny's Vocabulary of Shawnee
Volume 15. Cummings' Vocabulary of Delaware
Volume 16. Early Vocabularies of Mohawk
Volume 17. Schoolcraft's Vocabulary of Oneida
Volume 18. Elliot's Vocabulary of Cayuga
Volume 19. Schoolcraft's Vocabulary of Onondaga
Volume 20. Elliot's Vocabulary of Mohawk
Volume 21. Cummings' Vocabulary of Shawnee
Volume 22. A Vocabulary of Seneca
Volume 23. The Tutelo Language
Volume 24. Handy's Vocabulary of Miami
Volume 25. Observations on the Mahican Language
Volume 26. Minor Vocabularies of Tutelo and Saponi
Volume 27. Wood's Vocabulary of Massachusett
Volume 28. Chew's Vocabulary of Tuscarora
Volume 29. Early Fragments of Minsi Delaware
Volume 30. A Vocabulary of Wyandot
Volume 31. Heckewelder's Vocabulary of Nanticoke
Volume 32. Minor Vocabularies of Huron
Volume 33. Castiglioni's Vocabulary of Cherokee
Volume 34. Elements of a Miami-Illinois Grammar
Volume 35. Ridout's Vocabulary of Shawnee
Volume 36. A Vocabulary of Stockbridge Mahican
Volume 37. Minor Vocabularies of Nanticoke-Conoy
Volume 39. A Vocabulary of Etchemin
Volume 40. A Vocabulary of the Souriquois Jargon

For more information on the series, see our website at:
www.evolpub.com/ALR/ALRbooks.html

www.ingramcontent.com/pod-product-compliance
Lightning Source LLC
Chambersburg PA
CBHW021342090426
42742CB00008B/713